W9-AKD-290

BLACKLASH

How Obama and the Left Are
Driving Americans to the
Government Plantation

DENEEN BORELLI

THRESHOLD EDITIONS

New York   London   Toronto   Sydney   New Delhi

Threshold Editions
A Division of Simon & Schuster, Inc.
1230 Avenue of the Americas
New York, NY 10020

First Threshold Editions hardcover edition March 2012

THRESHOLD EDITIONS and colophon are trademarks of
Simon & Schuster, Inc.

For information about special discounts for bulk purchases, please
contact Simon & Schuster Special Sales at 1-866-506-1949 or
business@simonandschuster.com.

The Simon & Schuster Speakers Bureau can bring authors to your
live event. For more information or to book an event, contact
the Simon & Schuster Speakers Bureau at 1-866-248-3049
or visit our website at www.simonspeakers.com.

Designed by Renata Di Biase

Manufactured in the United States of America

10   9   8   7   6   5   4   3   2

Library of Congress Cataloging-in-Publication Data

Borelli, Deneen.
    Blacklash / Deneen Borelli.
      p.   cm.
       1. United States—Politics and government—2001–2009.   2. Obama,
Barack—Political and social views.   3. African Americans—Social
conditions—21st century.   4. United States—Race relations—Political
aspects—History—21st century.   I. Title.
    E907.B67   2012
    973.932—dc23   2011037104

ISBN 978-1-4516-4286-5
ISBN 978-1-4516-4288-9 (ebook)

To the defenders of liberty—past, present, and future

CONTENTS

BLACKLASH

BLACKLASH

INTRODUCTION

Hard Work, Not Handouts

One of the first links that comes up when you Google my name is an article entitled the "Black Tea-Bagging: 'Nigger' Deneen Borelli Please!" Note that it seems that the author believed it was not good enough to just identify me as black—I am a *black* and a *nigger*. The *black* is to let you know my skin color because apparently that will tell you something relevant about me. The second part, the *nigger* part, is to underscore the author's belief that I am something less than a white person. Not an American, not a freethinker, but subhuman: a *nigger*, because my racial and ethnic ancestry is broadly associated with slavery, degradation, and abusive treatment.

That's right, *my* long list of accomplishments and my position as a mentor and role model are not front and center. I am not referred to as a Tea Party activist or a noted conservative commentator. My entire life is reduced to one very ugly slur. Instead of questioning my ideas or thoughts, people attack me. Shoot the messenger so to speak. How pathetic. I am not a victim, but why am I their target?

And *black nigger* is not the only name I've been called. I could list dozens. As a result of my conservative views, I am targeted and called names by varying cowards who hide behind the anonymity of their computers and the Internet. Because I am black, because I am depicted as a *black nigger*, and because I am a woman who is not afraid to speak the truth, I have become a target for race-baiting, women-hating loons from across the political spectrum. Just check out some of the emails and tweets I get (spelling errors not mine!):

- "your a white bitch I trully trully hope someone jumps out and deals with you bitch."

- "You can not speak for black people, so take your Stepin Fetchit ass back to your master on the plantation. Get your head of your ass or out of Rush Limbaugh's ass."

- "Don't get mad, just sit quietly for a few minutes, go inside yourself and relive some of those moments. Now go find your parents and slap the shit out of them."

- "You are a despicable piece of garbage! A nigger crawling back to the plantation."

- "be honest with yourself and examine—you are being used by the New American Nazi Party, built on racial hatred and exclusion. Those people in attendance would slit your throat if they caught you in a back alley purely because of your skin tone."

Clearly my visibility as a conservative activist and on television, where I express the benefits of individualism, limited government, and liberty, threatens the radical fringe of the progressive movement whose policies are designed to limit individual liberty and keep black Americans on the government plantation. It also seems to confuse those people who like to send emails and tweet, but can't spell.

By now, you have probably figured out that I am a proud conservative. I believe in the power of the individual. I'm a freethinker and I love my country. Yes, I'm also black, but that fact has nothing to do with my belief in limited government. White people can be liberal or conservative. In fact, they are free to flirt with communism or socialism too. But why is it that they seem to have more choices than I am supposed to have? Why can't a black woman question the outrageous spending of our government? Why do people assume that if I am black, I should automatically endorse entitlement programs for the poor? If white people can question government handouts, why can't I question them too?

Here is another one of my so-called problems: I am

black and I don't like how the country's first black president does his job. Obviously, I don't dislike President Obama because he is *black*. Really, whether his skin color was black, white, or green is irrelevant to me. I don't like Obama because he is doing a horrible job as president. President Barack Obama's administration has advanced policies that are taking the country backward and his spending habits are out of control. But, some people apparently think that my economic concerns shouldn't supersede my ethnicity. There is this strange notion that because I am black I should agree with all black people. But all white people are not similarly expected to agree with Bill Clinton or George Bush. Nor are all women expected to agree with Hillary Clinton or Michele Bachmann. So why is it that black people—especially black women—aren't allowed to have their own opinions?

Let me set the facts straight. I don't agree with the president's $787 billion failed stimulus package. He says it was aimed at curbing the then 8 percent unemployment rate, but did he ever really think through the implications of it? Following these cash infusions, the jobless rate hit 10 percent. The plan was doomed from the beginning, because it went to save state budget shortfalls. Facing persistently high unemployment in September 2011 and with more than 14 million people out of work and fearing another recession, Obama went back to the progressive playbook and proposed a $474 billion mini-stimulus before a joint session of Congress. Honestly, what was this man thinking?

In fact, many white Americans didn't agree with Obama's spending and stimulus and big government initiatives. They didn't get called names. They weren't subjected to racial slurs because they took a stand against these initiatives. So why was I targeted? Why was I viewed as a "race traitor"?

I'm black and I don't agree with the policies and spending initiatives of a black president. Somehow that crossed a line in the sand: the belief that all black people share the same views because they share the same racial makeup.

Equally as problematic to some, my last name is Borelli. People believe that entitles them to question who I am. They ask "Is she really black? Or is she really black and just trying to be white?" Forget that hundreds of thousands of women take the last name of their husband—which is what I did. My maiden name is Moore. Apparently being black, having a last name such as Borelli and questioning the decision making of President Obama made me fair game for those that believe that race trumps ideas in politics.

I can take the name-calling, but not everyone can. Why should people who desire freedom and liberty have to endure being called racist because they disagree with the Obama administration and its policies? I realized just how difficult it was for others when I attended Glenn Beck's Restoring Honor event on the mall in Washington, DC, on August 28, 2010. It was there that I met a woman and her granddaughter from Houston, Texas. She was thrilled to meet me because of my ideas and concerns about big government. She thought I was a role model for her granddaughter.

I was moved. Here was a white woman from the South

looking to me for leadership. This encounter was important to me because it made me realize there was something very important about the Tea Party movement and our fight for the cause. For people like this lovely woman from Houston, who are engaging in politics to stand up for liberty, it hurts them to be labeled racist by the mainstream media and other critics in the country. It's a loaded word and nobody deserves to be told they're racist simply because they don't agree with Obama's policies. Clearly for this woman from Houston, I validate her cause because I'm black and I stand beside her. I share her beliefs of limited government, individualism, and freedom even though we're of a different race.

I was really touched by our encounter. It made me realize that all the work and effort that goes into what we do is worth enduring the attacks. Let those who want come after me if they believe that is the best way to defend government spending. If attacking me personally is their only position, then I am honored to take the hits from the other side to stand up for Americans and what is right.

My husband Tom and I travel a lot and work crazy hours, but our message is getting through. I'm a voice for people who don't have a voice and access to the media. They can't do what I do and can't say what we all want to say for fear of attack. And it isn't just the grandmother from Houston who has touched me in this way. I have had numerous responses and conversations from people whom I call *closet conservatives.* They hail from around the country, but they are often members of the black community. They support what I say, but for varying personal and professional reasons they can't freely express themselves because of the attacks they will endure.

I get emails and notes on Facebook after almost every television appearance I make. They come from a range of people but perhaps most significantly, they come from young black Americans who have been afraid to speak out because they come from a long line of left-leaning family and community members. They feel they are *supposed to be* Democrats, but they are black, conservative, and ready for change. They are our future and our hope for liberty. So many people are nervous to speak out, so I'm speaking out for them. I am not afraid to take on those who think limits to our liberty are justified. I don't care that Barack Obama is black, he is still hurting this nation, and someone has to stand up to that. My speeches, my work, and now this book are intended to help blaze a trail for the road to freedom.

I also don't like the way some of the old-school black leaders have created and perpetuated a message of victimization among their black constituents. This message is archaic, dated—and it's downright wrong. We don't need to live on the government plantation. We don't need government handouts—in fact they're bad for us. Remember one thing: There is nothing free about free money. Handouts engender dependency. They create and entrench poverty, not fix it. It doesn't matter if you are a black or white president creating entitlement programs to attract voters, it is a bad policy. All Americans need to stand up and fight against it.

It was early in my life that I learned I had to work hard for what I wanted and for my successes. I am a better person for having had to make my own way in life. This understanding of how the world works was best epitomized for me during a race in high school at a track and field meet.

I remember those 12.4 seconds probably more vividly than any other moment in my lifetime. It's like it just happened five minutes ago—that's how easily I can recall everything about that race. It was spring of my freshman year. I was representing Burlington City High School in New Jersey in the 100-yard dash at a track meet. To my right: Carol Lewis, soon-to-be Olympic athlete and sister of multi-gold medalist Carl Lewis. I was determined to beat her and when the gun sounded I thought I might just pull it off. I got out of the blocks well before anyone else did, and I could feel the space between the rest of the runners and me. I kept thinking to myself "I can do this, I'm ahead of everyone else . . . I can beat Carol Lewis." I remember hearing her footsteps behind me—she was closing the gap. The sound of her stride on the track made me run faster. Like a blur though, somewhere during that 12.4 seconds she ran past me and broke through the tape first. She beat me. But I had set a record in the 100-yard dash for my school and I was happy about that. I achieved something that day. I worked hard for my accomplishments and was proud of it. I learned that success is about doing your best and accomplishing your goals, not about medals and awards.

My career as an athlete likely could have continued. Whether I could have gone on competing at elite events or not is not the point. I didn't have a choice. Sure, I had the athletic skills and I was a top athlete in four track sports— 100-yard dash, long jump, high jump, and anchor leg in the 4×100 relay. And sure, if I could have competed in my senior year, I very likely would have had a scholarship to college. But it was not an option for me. I'd grown up in a middle-class home where a strong work ethic was instilled. My father was a security guard at a correctional facility during the day and worked at a supermarket at night. My mother was a secretary and a counselor. I knew I had to get a part-time job myself and start contributing. I had to work for what I wanted to buy—like my first car—and to give something to my parents for the household. It was time and I knew that. And that meant no track and field and likely no college either. That would have to come later.

I never really felt angry. Perhaps I was a little disap-pointed, but I saw it as my *sacrifice*. It was what it was. I never gave up on any of my dreams, just as I kept going in the race. I just knew I'd have to work for what I wanted in life and not depend on anyone. I had learned inher-ently that hard work paid off and I was going to get myself ahead in a career and think for myself as an individual.

That race and my family life and my work ethic have always stuck with me. I did go on to get my degree, but it took me eleven years of very hard work. I paid for it through an employee reimbursement fund from Philip

Morris, where I worked my way up the ranks for twenty years.

President Barack Obama and I are similar in that we faced family challenges during our upbringing, but through hard work and perseverance we overcame those liabilities. We worked hard for what we got and we were handed nothing extra without effort. We are both representative of much of the black community in the United States. While Michelle Obama may think she shares that experience, when I hear her whine about the *difficulties* of being black at Princeton University, I feel strongly that we do not share an experience at all. My experience was very different.

I didn't just *run* fast in high school. I learned to type fast—100 words per minute—and my shorthand was pretty impressive too. I got a full-time job at Philip Morris, first as a benefits clerk, and then over the years, as I worked hard, I was given more responsibility. No Ivy League for me.

I worked hard full-time, then took the subway from Midtown to Downtown during rush hour, cramming myself into crowded cars like a sardine in order to go to school part-time. All of this came after a full workday, so that I could attend classes in the evening. I would complete an eighteen-hour day, then get up the next morning to do it all over again. I spent weekends studying or trying to schedule group project time with my much younger fellow college students.

So allow me to laugh when our first lady complains about attending an elite Ivy League school on a full-time basis! Please—if all of us could have been so lucky! While I'm sure that being surrounded by predominately white elites at Princeton posed some challenges, it does not come close to the eleven-year marathon I endured.

When Philip Morris moved to Richmond, Virginia, I took the severance package after having worked there for twenty years. Instead I donated a year of my life to volunteer at the Congress of Racial Equality, one of the oldest civil rights organizations. Working at CORE I produced and cohosted a radio talk show called *The CORE Hour*. I had zero experience in public policy, because like many Americans I was too busy working to get involved in politics. Besides, public policy was for somebody else—none of what they do in Washington, DC, affects me . . . right?

While at CORE, I realized something: that almost everything I was exposed to growing up was wrong. The Reverends Sharpton's and Jackson's messages of bias, prejudice, victimization, and the need for special treatment simply did not match my life experiences. I was not a victim. No one has discriminated against me. I had God-given talents and it was up to me to make my own way and to be responsible for my decisions.

Maybe that's why I was able to make my own decision on Election Day 2008 and not vote by race. I think for a lot of black Americans—around 95 percent of the voting black population—that wasn't the case. Their racial association with Barack Obama meant they felt they had to vote for him when he ran—simply because he was black, because he was the first black candidate for president. That's simply the mindset among black people in this country.

The vote was based on racial pride to a certain extent. But it wasn't for me. I think people should vote not for the skin color of a person but for the character of that person and what he or she stands for, the principles he or she believes in and lives by. If you vote by character, you know a president will make choices while governing that reflect his or her character. If you vote for skin color alone, you're doing an injustice to yourself and to the country.

I didn't vote by the color of my skin or Obama's skin. I left race out of it. I did so because I had deep concerns about his left-wing views. The basic fact that in the U.S. Senate in 2007 he had the most liberal voting record of all senators—even more than Bernie Sanders of Vermont—was enough. As I am a conservative, that scared me.

Obama's radical influences were too much as well. His association with Reverend Wright was alarming. We have a sitting president who had a religious advisor who felt the need to say many outrageous statements, like "God damn America." That was not an association I felt comfortable with. I've been a practicing Christian my entire life, attending Baptist, Methodist, and now Roman Catholic services. In all the years I've gone to church, I have never heard radical statements such as Wright's from the pulpit. Nor was I okay with Obama's relationship with self-described communist and revolutionary Bill Ayers. My associates and contacts in the public policy sphere are individuals trying to improve our country's direction through the traditional routes like education. They are not using violent revolution by drawing on fringe elements as President Obama's circle has.

But what concerned me the most were the many ways in which Obama's overarching radical political philosophy seemed to find the Constitution a barrier for his activist government agenda.

According to Obama, our Constitution is deficient because it did not allow the government to take an active role in redistribution of wealth. During a 2001 interview with a Chicago radio station, Obama noted what he considered the failure of the Supreme Court to address economic justice. The Warren court, Obama said, "never ventured into the issues of redistribution of wealth, and of more basic issues such as political and economic justice in society."

Obama added, "It [the Court] didn't break free from the essential constraints that were placed by the Founding Fathers in the Constitution . . . that generally the Constitution is a charter of negative liberties. Says what the states can't do to you. Says what the federal government can't do to you, but doesn't say what the federal government or state government must do on your behalf." [1] Obama openly displayed the classic view of progressives that the Constitution is a barrier to their political agenda. [2]

He is a classic tax-and-spend liberal, and that has always been bad for the country. He made it very clear on the campaign trail and as a senator that he wanted to see the wealth of the nation redistributed.

Obama's earlier interest in wealth redistribution surfaced during the campaign. He indirectly told the now-famous Joe the Plumber, "It's not that I want to punish your success—I just want to make sure that everybody who is behind you—that they've got a chance at success too." Obama continued: "My attitude is that if the economy's good for folks from the bottom up, it's gonna be good for everybody." Nobody should be surprised by his economic platform, regardless of the state of the nation's finances when he was elected.

In fairness, his background, record, and radical philosophy were in full view if anyone bothered to look. For those who elected him: You got what you voted for. So I was not surprised when Obama sought to expand the role of government with his health care plan, widely spend our tax money with economic stimulus and bailouts, and punish us with higher energy prices through his cap-and-trade energy scheme.

Obama's political philosophy demanded an activist government to level the economic playing field, despite what the Constitution may say. These are among the many reasons I couldn't be influenced by race when I went to the polls.

For me, the Obama presidency *does* prove we've come a long way—but in a different way. The naysayer will tell you that black Americans are kept down, but from my standpoint, the very fact that Obama was elected demonstrates how far we have risen above the racism that plagued us decades ago. Obama's election should have put the race card to bed, but it didn't. It should have ended affirmative action, but it didn't. It should have been the end of the Al Sharptons and Jesse Jacksons as the voice of the black community, but that never happened either. All in all, the election of Barack Obama to the office of president should have changed this country's view of race. But it didn't.

During the 1950s and 1960s, the black community fought and died for equality in housing, jobs, and education. It was a horrible era and as a people, we fought hard for equality. Today, however, I believe strongly that if you are black in this country and you haven't yet achieved equality—it's not society that is the problem, it's you. You're not working hard enough or striving for what you want. Before blaming society or looking to government to be responsible for you and your family: look in the mirror. What choices did you make? Drop out of school? Hang out with the wrong crowd? Get involved in drugs or gangs? Is teen pregnancy the government's fault? No, young people should avoid engaging in risky sexual behavior.

That's why I've written this book. To speak out for what I believe in and to tell the leaders of this great nation that we don't need their handouts, we don't need to be treated like victims and we don't want to live on the government plantation. I want to see an end to the attitude that "you are entitled to be supported, and that the government is supposed to take care of you." It is up to the individual to take the initiative to seek out opportunities and be successful. We can't afford to sit around and wait for someone to drop success in your lap. My life experiences don't reflect the messages of victimization and special treatment the traditional black leaders stress to blacks. I want people to hear these messages, but to think and act on their own. I want this book to inspire. I want to encourage everyone to educate him or herself, read and learn about the Constitution, and understand that we all have a voice and it's time to use it.

ONE

The Good Ol' Government Plantation

I have two words for the old civil rights guard: *step aside*.

Your time has passed and your message is dated. These days you are doing more to hurt the black community than you are helping it. And in the process, you are dismantling the greatness of the American nation. You aren't just hurting blacks with your backward tactics, but the country itself. Your archaic initiatives and your self-serving agendas need to end. It's time to fix the United States, focus on the economy, and put your outdated 1960s agenda to bed—the civil rights initiatives that began over fifty years ago just don't apply to today's world. Unless by choice, we don't sit at the back of the bus anymore. Let me be clear—we appreciated what you did, but now your old guard message needs to be modernized because hanging on to it only benefits you and hurts everyone else.

Of course, I am talking about a long list of black leaders who understand and conceptualize today's problems by looking backward rather than forward. I am referring to Jesse Jackson, Al Sharpton, and New York's censured Democratic Representative Charles Rangel. They rose to prominence years ago by telling us that the poverty that plagued blacks was someone else's fault. Members of the black community who didn't have jobs, housing, or money to feed themselves could feel better about themselves knowing they were victims rather than failures.

But these public figures who are leading the black population down that path need to seriously rethink their approach to civil rights issues and update their commentary. Their self-serving agendas for power and control have been obtained by playing the race card and in some cases, by declaring blacks are victims in need of special treatment. In some instances, they've even turned their victimization message into a business—claiming they are going after corporations for their communities, then oddly, benefiting personally and professionally. In some cases, investigations of black politicians are racially motivated.[1]

It's time to fight the new fight, not the old one. It's time to drop the old rhetoric and update the cause. It's time to take some responsibility for our own actions. Let me be clear. If we want to move forward, the shackles of yesteryear's rhetoric needs to be broken down and recast. Black Americans are a great people with great potential. Sometimes, everyone needs a reminder: that individuals control our own destiny rather than playing the blame game to justify personal failures.

This country elected a black president. That alone should have put to rest the constant rants of discrimination and the overwhelming demands for affirmative action to rest. No quota system here. Obama got elected because he worked hard and promoted his policies in such a way as to garnish the most votes. This fixation on victimization—the decades-old vision that the plights of the black community are someone else's fault—needs to go.

Obama's election should have been a wakeup call to the traditional black leaders that their message was outdated. They should have taken a step back and reassessed their message of victimization and blame. The message needs to be recast. It should have either stopped Jesse Jackson and his friends in their tracks or perhaps forced them to strive for new relevance. So I have to ask myself—What are they thinking? Why aren't black leaders listening?

Here's the problem: They need to look at modern society in the twenty-first century and initiate new ways to address its problems. Surging welfare dependency in the black community, alcoholism, children continually being born into single-parent homes—these things plague this nation. And it is only getting worse because the numbers keep rising.

Their moniker and reason for fighting is supposedly "justice for everybody" but the only ones benefiting are the guys making the noise. They are all benefiting personally. It's upsetting that they've been able to get away with this. People despise how the old guard is doing business. It's simply wrong. There's a cost to all of this. By not spending political clout on the new fight, these guys are not espousing the benefits of liberty. They are not enlightening people, nor are they advancing them. Rather they are missing the message and trying to keep the rest of us in a time warp. Here's a suggestion: Why not use your power to encourage school choice to stop soaring dropout rates?

The old way isn't working so let's pursue a new way. The Democrats are beholden to special interest groups—the feminists, unions, trial lawyers, and environmentalists. Here's an example: Jackson joins the unions' fight so he can't advocate for school choice. He'd break the alliance. But with this closed-minded approach everybody suffers and windows of opportunity to try to advance people are lost.

These kinds of problems existed before my time and I watched them destroy families in my youth. I was fortunate as a child. I didn't grow up in an inner city. I always had clean clothes and food on the table. But some of my relatives in cities like Camden and Philadelphia had a tough time. As a child I remember visiting others and observing the less than desirable conditions they were living in. I remember multiple kids in a bedroom, from multiple fathers, in bad neighborhoods. I could identify who was struggling and who was living in a situation that I know and understand today is tough to see beyond. There were people who depended on others and I understood that.

But I don't understand why so much of that still exists today. Tragically, the numbers are getting worse for blacks trapped in inner cities. Why aren't black kids improving and growing at the same rate as their peers? My opinion: It's all in the message from the career black politicians who promote big government solutions that result in stagnation and government dependence. They are playing the blame game and using the race card as their ace in the hole to avoid accountability. Hey, blame your problems on race and don't take responsibility for your life, even when you mess it up. That's easier than providing solutions. And let's face it: it keeps these guys in business.

They are just repeating the old message—victimization: Those old faces aren't fighting for their constituents or the black community anymore—they're just causing them more problems. We are in crisis in this country—but it is an economic one. Fight to fix that problem rather than throwing up your hands and casting blame by using the "woe is me" rhetoric.

These race charlatans are fighting for their own personal and professional agenda. Their activities and media forays are out of self-interest. They have an obsessive need to stay in the limelight even when they have little to say. And in many instances, their time in the public spotlights seems to ensure they benefit financially.

Career politician Rangel and social activists like Jackson and Sharpton want to preserve their special status and maintain their public persona. It is not clear they have anything meaningful to say, but it certainly helps with their personal bottom lines. Their financial self-interests seem to trump the needs of members of the black community. Why aren't they benefiting? Why aren't they seeing the same gains in their lives? In fact, it is my opinion that these guys are repressing the very group they are supposed to be helping by promoting big government solutions. Their message no longer contains inspiration. In fact, their messages no longer contain value. They adhere to the status quo on issues like school choice and are reliant on the notion that the government should just throw money at the old and failing way of doing things.

THE OLD BLACK GUARD

I don't want to give the impression that I'm not appreciative of all that's been done in the name of civil rights for me and a nation of black Americans and other minorities. I'm aware there were many who stood, fought, and died before me and I am humbled by the efforts and sacrifices of leaders such as Dr. Martin Luther King, Jr. They accomplished a great deal and must be recognized for their achievements.

But today, not every fight is a civil rights fight. Simply because a black American gets scolded at work or even fired, it's not necessarily an issue of discrimination. It could be, for example, a performance issue. Once I came up against a white female executive who wanted to have me fired. I never considered it to be an issue about my race. That didn't dawn on me. The bottom line was that in this situation, this person just didn't like me. But for the record, I didn't like her either. It was pretty clear cut. But not once did I think it was about my race. I never accused her of racism. Why would I? The issue of my skin color wasn't at issue in this employment matter.

In other words, every time a company fails to hire a black firm or consultant, it doesn't mean it is showing racial bias. Maybe there were stronger alternatives. And by relying on that old message—the one that says that we're always victims and we deserve special treatment, we're encouraging poor behavior and diminishing the opportunity for real strides and successes.

There was a Pennsylvania school issue recently that really demonstrates this point. A special group was created to help lagging students who had low scores. It happened to be that most, if not all of the kids that were targeted for assistance in this program were black. They were given a mentor to help them a few minutes a day—same race, same sex.

I was pulled into a debate on this topic because everyone started screaming segregation and racism. Let's be clear: If the public ever truly thought we were segregating our schools the way they were segregated in the 1950s, there would be an uprising of monumental proportion. This program was meant to help struggling students achieve. If it helped, was it really worth all the attention and screaming of racism? The teachers were black and Hispanic—it wasn't even white teachers directly involved. It's a classic case of looking through a window in the 1950s to fix problems in 2011. In other words, we need to think in the present and experiment with new solutions that might actually help rather than simply play the blame game. Should we get mentors to help black students develop their skills, help themselves and become successful? Or should we let everyone with low test scores fail?

Part of the problem is the messenger. Let's start with Jesse. Jesse Jackson is delivering not just the wrong message—he is giving you a bad one. Along with Shirley

Chisholm, a black congresswoman who ran for president in 1972, he may very well have paved the way for President Obama to even consider making a run for the highest office in the land. By running for president in 1984 and 1988, Jackson may even have broken the ice for others.

But Obama didn't bring Jackson into his inner circle ahead of 2008 for a reason. Jackson was too identified as an agitator and has just one tune in his repertoire: the race song. Obama wanted to distance himself from that old, traditional folk song that framed black Americans as victims rather than a thriving community with enormous potential.

And Jackson didn't take the hint either. He didn't use this lesson to grow or progress. Instead, he decided to hold a grudge. Jackson was caught on a hot mike after or before a radio interview saying he wanted to cut Obama's "nuts off." He claims Obama talks down to black people! Are you kidding me? He holds a destructive, counterproductive race-relations harming grudge. Obama didn't want to be tied to the traditional black leadership because he knew it would tarnish his image.

Here's the problem: Jackson uses his public persona to portray himself as someone fighting for civil rights. This is his cause and his message has but one theme. Poor black people have been taken advantage of by whites who have denied them their civil rights and they should be compensated for all the bad things that happened during slavery. Jesse Jackson said, "All those years of work without wages are the foundations of America's wealth. America must acknowledge its roots in the slavery empire, apologize for it . . . and work on some plan to compensate."[2]

He shows up out of nowhere to march with the unions protesting in Wisconsin. This was not a race issue but that didn't stop Jackson from making it one. In an appearance on Fox News, during the union takeover of the Capitol protesting the loss of collective bargaining rights, Jackson explained, "They're going to escalate the protests—you will either have collective bargaining through a vehicle called collective bargaining or you're going to have it through the streets. People here will fight back because they think their cause is moral and they have nowhere else to go."[3]

People must have been dumbstruck by his statement. It looked like he might be calling for riots. Was Jackson in his right mind? He was throwing fuel on the fire—it was almost as if he were a professional agitator. The uncritical media dutifully followed him. He played to the cameras and they played to him, just like they always do.

Jackson compared Wisconsin governor Scott Walker to racist Democrat George Wallace. I clearly don't understand his point: Walker is facing huge debt burdens in his state and trying to address bloated benefits. Whether you agree with Walker's approach to the budget crisis or not, surely we can all agree that race is not on the table. What has George Wallace to do with this mess? Jackson even compared the labor conflict in Wisconsin to the civil rights movement. He invoked the name of Martin Luther King, Jr., saying it was his last work on earth to march for workers. In an effort to draw a parallel between unions and the civil rights movement he said:

"This is the week we went across the Edmund Pettus Bridge in Selma for the right to vote," he said. "We have gone from Wallace trying to deny us the right to vote to Walker trying to deny workers the right to bargain. We have gone from Wallace to Walker . . . Dr. King's last act on Earth was marching for workers' rights . . . When we march, we honor Dr. King. When we march multiculturally and multiracially, we honor Dr. King. When we march nonviolently, we honor Dr. King."[4]

It was all quite a leap.[5]

On his own exploitation tour, Jackson went to Ohio too. Inserting himself into the labor dispute keeps him part of the labor front group. He can't go after Obama, because he would alienate blacks who voted for Obama. So he's desperately seeking relevance. He throws anything into the pot that he can think of at these events— attacking Wall Street, overseas cheap labor—just to get the attention, as he struggles to stay relevant, in a post-black-president environment.

When people overspent on their homes and couldn't afford their mortgages, Jesse pulled out the race card, claiming the banks were taking advantage because of bias. Then he took to the streets and picketed Wall Street—asking that banker bonuses cover the losses. He even went so far as to suggest we need a second stimulus to bail out Main Street—meaning we bailed out Wall Street, let's bail out the people too. But the basic fact is that Jackson's presence draws media attention and he knows it. The issue of what's right and wrong doesn't seem to matter to him, because racial bias is always a strong accusation. It is intimidating because of his history of boycotts and corporate shakedowns. Play the race card and all eyes are on you. It doesn't matter if it is true or not. That is not its purpose. Make the allegation and *it* becomes the story. Truth be damned.

It is in this context that I have to really question whether or not this guy is making any strides for the betterment of the black community. What is he doing to help raise the standard of living? Rhetoric doesn't feed the masses. It lines the pocket of the speaker. Instead of promoting freedom and liberty, he's masking his efforts as issues for civil rights race relations. As a result, everyone is getting shaken down. Whites, blacks, Hispanics, the poor, and the rich alike are paying the price. And who benefits? Yeah, that's right—Jesse Jackson.

Let me go through a few examples of Jackson's art of the shakedown.

Often when Jackson goes after an organization in order to allegedly promote civil rights issues, he seems to get a contribution on the back end of the fight. For lack of anything better to do with his time, he stays relevant by continuing with the same dumb news cycle. Look at the Freddie Mac example. Suspicions persist about the embattled government-backed mortgage giant, which made many generous contributions to Jackson's Rainbow/PUSH Coalition. But it's curious how this donation originated. The president of the ethics watchdog group, the National Legal and Policy Center (NLPC), Peter Flaherty said, "Jesse Jackson's relationship with Freddie Mac began in 1998 when Jackson accused Freddie Mac of racial discrimination and encouraged major shareholders to sell their stock. Freddie Mac began financial support for Jackson's organizations and his criticism of Freddie Mac stopped."[6] Shocking isn't it? So, all is well in the world of race once a donation has been made? Seems so because that's what it took in this instance to stop Jackson from going after Freddie Mac.

Even more incredible, Jackson continued to take money right around the time the country's economy was collapsing and the foreclosure rate was soaring. In light of the collapse of the mortgage market in this country, it's pretty shocking to learn that Jackson was somehow even benefiting financially right around the time Americans were losing their homes. Freddie Mac most recently donated $150,000 to a Rainbow/PUSH conference in August of 2008,[7] even as Congress was debating a bailout of the struggling firm that the Congressional Budget Office (CBO) projected might cost taxpayers as much as $100 billion.[8]

Then there's a sixteen-year crusade led by Jackson against Anheuser-Busch for not having enough minority beer distributors. Jackson went after the beer king because there were complaints that black employees at distributors weren't getting a sufficient number of promotions. The beer giant caved because it was afraid of a boycott. They tamped it down because Jackson could really start something and he had then-President Bill Clinton's ear. That also seems to have ended in a pay-off for Jackson's sons. They were awarded a lucrative Chicago distributorship despite questionable experience and financial backing.[9] And where did the money come from to buy it? Well, they never disclosed it and it was all kept quiet from the media.

Jackson attacks corporations under the guise of fighting for equal opportunities for black employees and organizations, but businesses that Jackson has continually criticized—including Toyota and NASCAR—all of a sudden become sponsors of his annual Wall Street Conference.[10] And then he eases up on the heat.

Jesse Jackson's shakedown strategy is nothing new. He seems to have been extorting money for silence for a long time. It's quite ironic actually that for more than a generation, he has been both a thorn in the side of corporate America and yet at the same time, a favorite beneficiary of big-business charity.

He's gotten such a reputation for these self-serving shenanigans, that Kenneth Timmerman, an investigative reporter, wrote an entire book on just this very topic. *Shakedown: Exposing the Real Jesse Jackson* provides eye-opening details about Jackson's life and his rise to fame and fortune. The author says that Jackson "has used the same basic techniques—refining them as he went along— of intimidation, coercion, and protection. In so doing he has enriched his family, steered billions of dollars of business to his friends, and launched a political dynasty."[11]

Timmerman concluded that "like other demagogues, [Jackson] has a troubled relationship with the truth, even a complete lack of interest in it. He invents, then embroiders, embellishes, and expands, and few ever have the courage to expose him." [12]

NLPC's Flaherty has gone so far as to liken Jackson to a "civil rights paper tiger"—alleging that Jackson's power is derived from a reputation he has built in the hallways of big business rather than the communities he claims to represent. In a 2006 interview on the Washington Post Radio website, Flaherty said "Jesse Jackson is not supported financially by African-Americans. He's a creature of corporate America. The Wall Street Project and its sister conference—takes place in Chicago in the summer—called the Rainbow/PUSH Citizenship Education Fund annual conference—are fund raising vehicles for Jesse Jackson's organizations—that's all they are. It's all corporate support—95 percent of the support comes from decision makers who are white, rich, and male. And that's Jesse Jackson's constituency." [13]

The list is almost endless. Jackson benefited by playing a key role in the merger between Travelers Group and Citicorp in the late 1990s too.[14] CEO Sanford I. Weill of Travelers Group sought Jackson's help to eliminate the Glass-Steagall Act, a Depression-era law that prevented insurance and brokerage firms from merging with banks. Jackson's support was needed since many black organizations opposed the mergers because they feared the new companies would not meet the total obligations established under the Community Reinvestment Act (CRA) for inner city development.[15] Still, Jackson struck a deal with Phil Gramm, then chairman of the Senate Banking Committee. Charlie Gasparino wrote about the deal saying, "Jackson agreed not to oppose another piece of legislation Gramm was pushing, and Gramm agreed to terminate Glass-Steagall once and for all."[16]

For his efforts, Weill secured legal help and fund raising support for Jackson's organizations.[17] Jesse Jackson effectively became a toll collector here. To get past him, you have to give him money. But how did Jesse Jackson, the supposed spokesperson for black rights, get to helping to eliminate Glass-Steagall? How does that make any sense? How did the community he was supposedly fighting to help benefit from terminating Glass-Steagall?

Jackson puts his family, friends, and his self-interest ahead of community interest. For example, by threatening a boycott of PepsiCo, Jackson was able to secure a role for his friend's investment bank in the Pepsi Bottling Group IPO (initial public offering).[18] Jackson's longtime buddy Chester Davenport also did okay as a result of Jackson's shakedown methods. Jackson used his influence to steer business deals Davenport's way. Davenport was enriched by Jackson in the past through the Ameritech and SBC merger. In the 1990s, Jackson's opposition to the merger ended when Davenport—with no previous telecom experience—became a partner in part of the sale of Ameritech's wireless business to GTE. The subsequent merger of GTE and Bell Atlantic was a financial gain for Jackson's Citizen Education Fund given that approximately $1 million in donations was received from both companies.

Jackson and Davenport also teamed up to try to take advantage of the merger of Sirius Satellite Radio and XM Satellite Radio. Jackson and Davenport jointly opposed the merger claiming the combined company would be a monopoly and restrict minority ownership of radio programming.[19, 20]

According to the *Washington Post*, Davenport explained that if regulators give the marriage a green light, the combined company should be required to turn over some channels to a minority-controlled entity and was hoping that Georgetown Partners would fill that role.[21] In their view, this proposal would address the monopoly concerns and provide ownership to a minority-controlled entity.[22] This greatly benefited Davenport's minority-owned private equity firm Georgetown Partners.[23] According to the *New York Times* in an article on April 12, 1999, Davenport acknowledges he got a piece of the Ameritech Corporation's $3.3 billion sale of half of its wireless telephone business, at least in part, because he is black. Not only that, in addition to being very likely the wealthiest black entrepreneur in the country with a net worth of $100 million, he still cries victimization. In that same story he is quoted as saying, "I think if I were white, I would own one of these damn telephone companies." The article and interview exposes "a revealing window on a new sort of corporate affirmative action that people from the Rev. Jesse Jackson to C. Michael Armstrong, chairman of the AT&T Corporation, are seizing on to bring blacks into the traditionally white worlds of telecommunications and finance."[24]

What bothers me about this affair and pattern is that

the race card was used in order to justify interference in the free market when race really didn't seem to be an issue at all. There shouldn't be special treatment here for some people—minorities or otherwise—who want to benefit from other people's businesses. The marketplace should determine who gets contracts or who gets promotions or a distributorship. It should be based on merit. You're holding management and shareholders hostage. Consumers will have to pay more for less. This increases racial tensions, not diminishes them.

Jackson attended several Federal Communications Commissions (FCC) hearings to voice his disapproval of the merger. According to a transcript from the October 31, 2007, meeting, Jackson said, "Stopping media consolidation is the most important way to help minority ownership." Jackson further noted, "If a giant company is able to purchase a station across the country, people of color already victims of the long history of discriminatory practices, lending practices, now the mortgage [inaudible] crisis, are pushed off the field, often out of the picture."[25] The FCC approved the merger in July 2008 with conditions including a requirement that 8 percent of their channel capacity be dedicated for noncommercial and minority programming.[26]

But my most up close and personal view of Jackson's antics came at the 2008 annual shareholder meeting of the JPMorgan Chase & Company financial services firm where I observed Jackson in action and made my own stand against him. During the question-and-answer session, Jackson pressed JPMorgan CEO Jamie Dimon about the company's commitment to diversity. Jackson asked Dimon how much of the $750 million spent on a recent merger went to minority contractors. As Jackson bluntly put it: "How much of that was done by black and brown lawyers?"[27]

While Dimon could not specify a dollar amount, he emphasized that JPMorgan's support of minority contractors has increased, as has the percentage of minorities in senior management positions. Dimon likely wasn't surprised to see Jackson at the mike. In February 2008 Jackson called Dimon about JPMorgan's role in the then-upcoming initial public offering of credit card giant Visa Inc.[28]

In a follow-up letter to Dimon, Jackson wrote "As you know, the IPO is expected to be the largest in U.S. history, raising up to $20 billion for VISA and generating over $350 million in fees to the investment banking firms involved in the deal. . . . It is our understanding that just four minority firms are involved in the IPO syndicate at the third tier level, none as co-managers or even junior co-managers. . . . This is a major step backward for Wall Street and its commitment to inclusion. . . . There must be some sense of 'equanomics' [a Jackson term marrying "racial justice" to "economic equality"] in the IPO deal— which the representation of minority investment banking firms compares favorably to our consumer use of credit cards."[29]

We don't need "equanomics." The black community needs free market initiatives that would allow competition, grow the economy, and increase jobs, which are badly needed. This concept of equanomics does the opposite. Jesse-bonics, Ebonics, we don't need made-up buzzwords. We need *jobs*.

To increase the political pressure on Dimon, Jackson sent a similar letter to Congressman Barney Frank (D-MA) and Senator Chris Dodd (D-CT), chairman of the Financial Services Committee and chairman of the House and Senate Banking Committee, respectively, each concluding with "We hope that your committee might address these issues through congressional hearings, and identify and seek reasonable remedies." [30]

Frustrated by what appears to me to be a long history of Jackson using semi-subtle campaigns to pressure corporations to donate, I spoke up at the JPMorgan shareholder meeting in May 2008. After Jackson spoke, I took his place at the microphone and asked Dimon and his board: "Will there ever be a day where you will stand up and say 'No' to Mr. Jackson and to his demands and messages of victimization and divisiveness? This is the United States of America, and this is not the 1960s. People should be hired based on their talents and they should be retained based on their results. There should not be color-coded hiring in the United States." [31]

Shareholders clapped. But, unlike Jackson's, my question went unanswered. [32] This kind of racial pressure is tough for a corporation to deal with. They should fight back because their sole responsibility is to represent shareholder interests. Unfortunately, they take the easy route because they don't want to be embroiled in a public relations battle with Jackson. CEOs are afraid because Jackson can flick a switch and start a boycott and cost a company millions of dollars. People will do what they are told without really reading the fine print or understand the motivation of a guy like Jesse Jackson. So, corporations fear the blowback and Jackson milks that fear, builds his power, and sits back and waits for a check.

REVEREND AL SHARPTON

If Jesse Jackson is a corporate shakedown artist, Al Sharpton is an ambulance chaser.

He's grabbed his power by making sure no matter what issue is happening, whatever the crisis may be, he brings race to the table—warranted or not. Anything said about race is very powerful. Headlines follow whether or not the racial comments are true or false. The problem is, this sort of approach keeps guys like Al Sharpton in business. There is no accountability so Sharpton, like Jackson, maintains his 1960s view of the world to hold onto his power. If he recognized that modern society has changed, he'd lose his power and influence. The biggest problem: the collateral damage to his community left in the wake. There are many examples of Sharpton doing more harm than good by screaming "racial discrimination."

Look back to 1987 when a young girl named Tawana Brawley claimed she was repeatedly raped and left in a garbage bag near her apartment covered in feces, her body covered in racial slurs. She said her rapists were a group of white men, but a grand jury determined she was never actually assaulted. To this day, Tawana and her family maintain she was in fact assaulted. It's impossible to assess what really happened and if the grand jury was accurate, the fallout of this sad tale is even more troubling. The really horrible part of the story is the unnecessary exploitation that followed. Ambulance-chasing Al Sharpton grabbed on to this girl and became one of her advisors— he screamed racial discrimination and everything else he could think of to get the national spotlight on this case. Simply put, he exploited her to grab a platform from which to shout—his own self-interests coming first. And the aftermath was terrible. Sharpton's actions placed her in a worse situation, and in the process enhanced the racial tension and personal misfortunes of the accused. It's fair to say, there are times when discretion and simple courtroom justice are a better approach to finding the truth than the race-card pulpit.[33, 34]

As soon as Sharpton is involved, consider a situation blown out of proportion. This girl's story got bigger because of his pressure. In fact, it became a landslide and many lives were ruined as a result.

A more recent example of Sharpton's burning desire for the spotlight is a bit perplexing and somewhat offensive. In the wake of the January 2011 shooting of Representative Gabrielle Giffords at close range during an event at an Arizona mall, Sharpton seized an opportunity.

This shooting, which took six lives, spurred Al Sharpton to pen an opinion piece for the *Washington Post* recalling a time in 1991 he was stabbed during weeks of protests following the killing of a black teen in New York. He said,

There were incidents of taunts, people throwing watermelons and open threats. I was leading a peaceful march in Bensonhurst, Brooklyn, when I was stabbed. I look at that stab wound every morning. It reminds me of how close I came to leaving my children fatherless—all because of the intense political climate of the day. I wrestled for months with how to address that climate and the race-based attack. Even though this was an effort to kill me, I asked the court for leniency toward my assailant. In the spirit of King's teachings, my focus was to set a tone of forgiveness and reconciliation. Despite my efforts, the judge sentenced this man to nine years.[35]

The only thing he had to draw upon was a stabbing that happened thirty years ago, to him. His statements didn't feel healing; rather, they paint him as a narcissist with nothing new or relevant to say at a very emotional time in our nation's history.

His reference to crossing a line was about a situation many years ago in Harlem, in which a white business owner was trying to evict the original black business owner of his shop on 125th Street. Sharpton joined the protests to save the black-owned store and referred to the "white" businessman by race. Weeks later, someone set fire to the white-owned shop and lives were lost; another example of the need for Sharpton to stop digging into his arsenal of 1960s tools and firing off racial epitaphs. His rant caused harm. His detractors, I note, have said that his actions are potentially racist on their own.[36]

The Giffords shooting incident represented a chance for Sharpton to resume another old fight in order to draw attention to him. Giffords was shot, but Sharpton wants to be the news. So he has been going after the Federal Communications Commission to keep so-called racist content off the airwaves as part of the Giffords shooting. He has ramped up his calls to regulate racism in broadcasting. Talk about finding a way to insert yourself into the national dialogue when the story has nothing to do with you (or race)! If Giffords had a chance to respond, what would she say of Sharpton's involvement in her shooting? Sharpton appears to be capitalizing on the tragedy that wasn't race related.

Sharpton has been hounding the FCC on this topic for a while. He's been after the commission to increase airwave regulation. He wants comments that could be construed as racist to be treated the same way as cursing and nudity would be treated. His main target seems to be Rush Limbaugh, who, it seems, he'd like to see taken off the airwaves. A report in TheHill.com said, "Sharpton has singled out Limbaugh's comments comparing President Obama's policies to 'reparations' as potentially racist. 'We're not telling Rush don't say what he wants to say. Say it at home,' Sharpton said. 'Don't get on publicly regulated radio and television that are selectively given licenses and do that to offend someone because of their race or their gender.'"[37]

And Obama's political allure for Sharpton is likely enhanced since MSNBC made Sharpton a host for the daily evening show *PoliticsNation.* Sharpton's rise to TV host surprised some, but then again he took an active role in lobbying for the approval of Comcast's purchase of NBCUniversal, the parent company of MSNBC.[38]

Regardless of how Sharpton got the post, what better position can Obama ask for than to have a political ally spinning the White House messages cloaked as news? I can see the stories now—Tea Party racists, class warfare, and more government spending!!

Sharpton's critics are clear: They claim he has actually set race relations back a very long way. Academic and sociologist Orlando Patterson has referred to Sharpton as a racial arsonist and others have compared him to Richard Nixon and Pat Robertson. Why is Al Sharpton Obama's political ally? Is it a coincidence that soon after Obama harshly criticized Arizona's immigration law Sharpton leads a protest rally at the state's capitol? I don't think so![39]

Activists from the Hispanic Federation, like Lillian Rodriguez Lopez, might have been smarter to separate from this has-been when announcing the launch of a legal challenge to fight the bill that allows detaining of anyone in Arizona. Sharpton pulled out the old civil disobedience play from his civil rights handbook to join the fight there.[40]

Why is Al Sharpton the person Obama sends to Arizona to rally against that state's immigration crackdown? It was a smart move on the part of Obama—a clear campaign strategy. Let Sharpton create a circus-like atmosphere to ensure the issues get buried. Obama lets Sharpton make lots of noise and then he never has to take a position on the issue one way or another. Let's not kid ourselves—Obama won't be seen on the campaign trail with Sharpton when the chips count.

It's ironic because Obama wanted nothing to do with Sharpton during the 2008 presidential election. But now in a troubled economy, Obama may need Sharpton to keep black voters in line for the upcoming presidential election. Maybe this union between Obama and Sharpton will be the beginning of something more. Obama will let Sharpton take the hits, be the front man on controversial issues. Obama can let Sharpton play the race card and deflect attention away from his miserable handling of the country's economy.

It is a problem that Obama goes to these levels. And the Tea Party movement knows full well the damage it causes to our liberty. Sharpton's carnival-like rallies on race, among other things, help to distract the black community from seriously questioning the fundamental policies of the Obama administration.

Obama might be subtly wading one step toward the old guard's way. With poll numbers dropping, he seems to be leaning to use Sharpton on some missions and not just in Arizona. In April 2011, the president, for the first time since taking office, spoke at the annual convention of the National Action Network, alongside the organization's founder, one Al Sharpton. Obama had pretty much ignored Sharpton up until this point, but with those poll numbers slipping among blacks, maybe the president needs to look both to the old school and forward to get reelected.[41]

AN OVER-SERVED TERM

If aliens came down and looked at our cities, they'd wonder what was going on. How can politicians who claim to be acting in the interests of their people be benefiting so much? One of the greatest examples of an over-served term is the one held by Representative Charles Rangel in Harlem. Rangel is the houseguest who never leaves—the career politician who needs to move along and retire. He lives in a region riddled with crime, poor-testing schools, and extreme poverty. And what's this guy doing? Evading taxes, lying, and benefiting personally and financially off of the backs of his constituents. He's fulfilled his own personal needs, exploited the system, and put himself ahead of the people who need his representation. This isn't Beverly Hills. This guy is ripping off the poor people who need his help. His gains over the years have well outpaced theirs. And if you are questioning my characterizations, let me suggest someone else's thoughts on the issue. Ask the Democrats themselves what they think. It's not like it is a secret or anything: "By its adoption of House Resolution 1737, the House is resolved that representative Charles Rangel of New York be censured," Nancy Pelosi read, calling on the fallen chairman of the Ways and Means committee to pay the taxes he owes.[42]

How has he managed to do this for so long? First, you

have to honor Rangel for his service in the United States Army, for which he earned a purple heart. So at one point early in his career, he actually did some good for his community. But he has been serving his district since 1971 and the world today is very different. Despite having been censured by the House, this eighty-year-old career politician is shamelessly making another 2012 run.[43]

Look at the ethics violations he has been found guilty of: He was evading taxes by not declaring rental income from his vacation home in the Dominican Republic for seventeen years. He used his office to help raise money so he could have a building named after him at City College New York. Rangel's poor judgment is the reason he was censured by the House Ethics Committee—one of only twenty-two in congressional history to receive such a penalty.[44]

But the most outrageous Rangel violation came at the expense of a poor community and its people: Rangel had been improperly renting several rent-stabilized Manhattan apartments—four in fact. One was even being used as an office, which according to local and state regulations, are pretty clearly meant to be used as a primary residence if in fact they're rent stabilized. And his other three, his Harlem apartments, which he was enjoying while his constituents struggled to find affordable living cost him under $4,000 a month—half their market value.[45] If anyone can afford to pay the market price, it's Rangel. How does this help the constituents he has sworn to serve? He's taking from them the very thing they fight to have. There's no struggle for him.[46]

Not that any lessons were learned. The message Congress sent Rangel when the House voted by a wide margin, 333–79, to censure him was short lived. Within a year the House honored Rangel for his service in a ceremony unveiling a portrait of him that will be displayed in the Capitol. Keeping with his entitlement mentality, the $64,000 portrait was paid for with campaign funds. In 2007, Rangel complained about the lack of diversity displayed in paintings in the Capitol saying, "the only black folks I see are slaves holding the goddamn horses." Censuring, then honoring, a disgraced colleague illustrates the frustration of many Americans with Congress. It should come to no surprise that congressional approval ratings are in the single digits.[47]

Before being humbled and demoted by his missteps, Rangel, when still the chairman of the House Ways and Means Committee, was your run-of-the-mill, race-card playing politician. He maintained that the reason there was serious opposition to President Obama's healthcare plan was because the president is black.

That's right—"bias" and "prejudice," not the outrageous cost of the plan, its considerable red tape, and its messed-up nature. It was allegedly about race. Again, it was a has-been politician pulling out the only play he has in his arsenal to insert himself into a national dialogue. Talk about being far off mark from what was truly at the crux of health care. Rangel actually went so far as to compare the debate over health care to the war for civil rights. He said, "Why do we have to wait for the right to vote? Why can't we get what God has given us? That is the right to live as human beings and not negotiate with white southerners and not count the votes. Just do the right thing."[48]

He wasn't alone in the empty rant that Obama was struggling to get healthcare through because he's black. Then New York governor David Paterson also played the race card to explain why Obama's health care plan was facing challenges. This shouldn't come as a surprise to anyone. Paterson used the race card to explain away his political misfortunes as well. Paterson said, "The reality is the next victim on the list—and you can see it coming—is President Barack Obama, who did nothing more than trying to reform a health care system."[49] Paterson blamed the media's racism for pushing him out of running for a second term, not his utter failure to lead his state. Then Representative Diane Watson made a similar claim too, even going one step further: Michelle Malkin was kind enough to post online the transcripts of a Watson speech courtesy of KABC, which Malkin claims add to the race-baiting nature of this politician. Malkin prefaced the transcript by saying, "Bring an airsickness bag before reading."

WATSON: You might have heard their philosophical leader. I think his name is Rush Limbaugh. And he said early on, "I hope that he fails."

Do you know what that means? If the president, your commander-in-chief, fails, America fails.

Now, when a senator says that this will be his

Waterloo, and we all know what happened at Waterloo, then we have him and he fails. Do we want a failed state called the United States?

And remember: They are spreading fear and they are trying to see that the first president that looks like me fails.

Now just understand what's at the bottom line.

And you know we just got, 48 hours ago, we just go back, we were in Beijing, China, Hong Kong, China, we were in Taiwan, we were in Guam, we were all over the Far East.

I just want you to know: People look at the United States as a country that has changed its way and has elected someone from Kenya and Kansas, I'll put it like that.

And they're saying, "We thought you would never do that."

So we don't want to have this young man, and he just turned 48—we want him to succeed, because when he succeeds, we regain our status. We regain our status.

It was just mentioned to me by our esteemed speaker, "Did anyone say anything about the Cuban health system?"

And lemme tell ya, before you say "Oh, it's a commu—," you need to go down there and see what Fidel Castro put in place. And I want you to know, now, you can think whatever you want to about Fidel Castro, but he was one of the brightest leaders I have ever met. [APPLAUSE]

And you know, the Cuban revolution that kicked

out the wealthy, Che Guevara did that, and then, after they took over, they went out among the population to find someone who could lead this new nation, and they found . . . well, just leave it there (laughs), an attorney by the name of Fidel Castro . . .[50]

THE SLAVE TRAITORS

Rangel, Jackson, and Sharpton—clinging to their fleeting moment in the spotlight—are using the race card to promote their own interests. If they want to help the black community improve their standard of living, their employment status, and education, they'd be helping them help themselves. Freedom and liberty allow an individual to succeed. Government handouts engender dependency. Stop preaching the false claims that blacks are victims. They are a community of enormous potential and significance, capable of great things.

Rangel, Jackson, and Sharpton are very blatantly focusing on self-interest by entrenching the status quo. And guess what? They all get to keep their jobs that way. If we recognize the world has changed over the past several decades, their message will expire and they won't have much left to stand on.

If they want to support their fellow black Americans, they need to stop being traitors to their own people.

TWO

The Obama Irony

And let me tell you something: For the first time in
my adult lifetime, I'm really proud of my country.

—*Michelle Obama*

nlike Michelle Obama, I was proud to be American
can long before we elected a black president. Looking at what our president is doing to the country,
well, that I'm not so proud of. When historians assess
President Barack Obama's legacy, there will be an unmis-
takable irony to it. Yes, he will have been the first black
president elected in the United States, but *his* story, long
after he has left office, will be about how he created op-
pression in America through the failure of his progressive
policies. The black community will be the net losers, not
winners, of the first black president in American history.
The irony of his presidency will be based on his misguided

notions expressed through his policies: that collectivism trumps individualism and that an all-knowing government with legions of bureaucrats is the best arbitrator of economic resources. He's shown us these are his beliefs through ObamaCare, stimulus, and command and control energy policies.

It was indeed an overwhelming majority of black voters that swept Obama into office. An estimated 95 percent[1] of black voters participated in the excitement of electing the first black president. In some ways, many viewed it as the black community's victory as much as Obama's. One of their own was elected to the country's highest office.

Yet, Obama's support has slid substantially since the 2008 campaign. Not just among white voters, but the black community that swept him into power. As Gallup results indicate, more and more people are questioning his leadership. In April 2009, 73 percent of Americans viewed him as a strong and decisive leader while just two years into his presidency the figure stood only at 52 percent.[2] Moreover, Obama's "job approval rating fell from 58 percent to 47 percent between 2009 and 2010" with states like Wyoming only giving him a 28 percent approval rating.[3] Much of the criticism of his presidency pertains to his lackluster performance on the economy. A February 2010 poll demonstrated that "Six in 10 Americans (60 percent) believe that President Barack Obama has not devoted enough time to economic problems" while only "33 percent say he has spent the right amount of time on the issue."[4]

How ironic is it that the man that touted "Yes, we

can" can't hold on to the momentum that swept him to office. In only a two-year period, the presidency of *hope* and *change* has become one of *dread* and *status quo*. With strong approval ratings when he took office, Obama had enough tail wind to achieve almost anything. The problem, however, was not his color but his philosophy and promise to "Fundamentally transform the United States of America." His plan went against the tide of what has made America great. I think America has now awakened to the fact that he was taking us in the wrong direction from the beginning. Instead of advancing policies that would help the less fortunate rise out of poverty to achieve economic success through economic liberation, he charted a very different course.

After all, President Obama knows from experience that America truly is the land of unlimited opportunity if individuals are allowed to empower themselves. Liberty, not big government, permits us to meet our potential.

SPENDING OTHER PEOPLE'S MONEY

Early into his presidency, Obama racked up some historic spending figures. There was the $3.9 trillion in spending for 2009 and similar projections for 2010, but the historic levels of national debt were the scarier number: Just three months into his term, the nation faced levels not seen before—a staggering $11 trillion. That's almost half a trillion more than on the day he took office. The projections from his budget were even greater for 2012 (the year he hopes to get reelected!): The country, under President Obama, will face $16.2 trillion dollars in debt. Who is going to pay that bill? Numbers like that don't free Americans. Ironically, numbers like that saddle our children with bills to pay, bills that will keep the underclass on the government plantation for years to come.

Barack Obama's rise to the office of president of the United States from a single-parent household should have made life easier for struggling Americans. Instead his policies will make it more challenging, if not impossible for the less fortunate to gain upward mobility. He's bankrupting the country and its people, he's expanding and entrenching the bureaucracy and he's drawing a roadmap for Americans to live a life of government dependency. The Obama welcome mat for working-class Americans should read: *Welcome to a country that discourages advancement, entrepreneurialism, and self-fulfilled achievement.* Welcome to a country that, in essence, wants you and your family on a government run plantation for decades to come.

The Obama approach to running the country has a certain irony to it. He faced the similar obstacles and challenges so many other black Americans face today in that he was raised largely without a father with his grandparents doing much of the rearing. He didn't get an easy start by having a family name like Kennedy or Bush. Yet despite the difficulties, he still achieved the ultimate American Dream. He rose out of nothing and landed in the Oval Office.

But the numbers speak for themselves. Under the Obama administration, unemployment is still soaring and more than 46 million Americans get food stamps in order to feed their families. Nearly 460,000 jobs have gone away—evaporated—and despite many promises to create new ones, none of Obama's vast number of policy initiatives has moved that number much. We are hearing a lot about a "double dip recession" too. And how about this: Recent government data shows that less than half of the population of black teens in America have jobs.[5]

Across the country, moms and dads are desperate for help with shelter, clothing, and the bare necessities. In 2009, in Detroit, a city devastated by the recession and declining auto sector, tens of thousands of people stood in the bitter cold for days waiting for government to help them meet their basic housing and utility needs. However, the grants were only enough to assist an estimated thirty-five hundred families. The system is bursting at the seams in Atlanta as well, where the need for Section 8 Housing is so great that recently thirty thousand applicants stood in line in the hot summer just to get on a *waiting* list. A mortgage modification plan in hard-hit Florida brought twenty thousand applicants out seeking help in a five-day period. The problems and dependence are only going to get worse. Obama is creating oppressive policies and a vast number of them: stimulus, overregulation and over spending.

The irony, of course, is the consequences of his policies will take opportunities away from those who face similar challenges. Too bad he isn't going to let millions of Americans reach their dreams too. Too bad he isn't turning into the role model so many had hoped he'd become. Obama should have been the president who proved that in

America anyone could become anything with hard work and focus and a belief in individualism. Instead, he and his administration, through policies, stimulus, and the cronyism, are entrenching status quo politics whereby the rich get richer, on the backs of hardworking Americans.

It shouldn't be like this. We live in a great nation with an abundance of human and natural resources. We should be doing better. But we are approaching the problem incorrectly. The solution doesn't lie in handing out more assistance. Giving food away, providing temporary shelter, and handing out vouchers for utilities are little more than Band-Aid solutions. Why? Because next month the same people will still be living well below the poverty line. Nothing has changed for them except the freebies they received last month need to be replenished this month.

We need to stop the cycle of dependency that Obama's policies are unleashing. We need to reverse his *dependency politics* approach to governance and look for leadership elsewhere. We need to stop the migration of Americans to the government plantation and start recognizing that handouts are a life sentence of poverty. The dependency approach that Washington elites want to entrench will only ensure that poor Americans remain poor for generations to come.

We need to revisit the current policy approaches to remove the air of uncertainty. Government should be about creating an environment that allows for individuals to pursue economic prosperity. It should be about creating a pro-business climate to ensure job creation is flourishing. We need to make sure that manufacturers want to put their companies in the United States because our workforce and our resources are second to none. We need an energy policy that will encourage development of our natural resources, provide jobs, and needed tax revenue. We need to create a tax environment that works for CEOs rather than against them. And most importantly, we need to help the American people realize that getting handouts will only hurt them in the long run, that they need to use their own skills and hard work to get ahead.

Ironically, it is the government that creates the need for government assistance. The Obama administration is responsible for creating a path to greater dependency. The country must reduce the public's need for handouts. We don't want Americans to spend their lives scrounging for basic needs. The government should create a political and economic climate that will ensure people can provide for themselves and stand on their own two feet. This is what Americans want and this is what our president should want.

STATUS QUO POLITICS

Instead, Obama and Washington's elite are entrenching status quo politics. They are wedded to that big government agenda because their friends benefit so much. Let's look at what ObamaCare is doing to the country's bottom line: According to a congressional panel report, we're going to get slammed with $569 billion in higher taxes to pay for health care that won't really help the majority of

Americans. We're going to see cuts as high as $529 billion to the Medicare system.[6]

And talk about red tape: Two new government bureaucracies are being created to control the system. Not only will we spend loads of cash to hire more policy drones to staff these departments, but also they will create more red tape to effectively block people that are trying to get help. And these mandates to insurance companies are too complicated. They are lengthy and will just add to the costs.

If you're wondering why the pharmaceutical companies aren't crying out in opposition to this plan, just remember one thing. It is they, not the American people that are going to benefit from ObamaCare. They will gain billions of dollars in new revenue from all the newly insured people going to doctors and filling prescriptions.[7] Big Pharma spent nearly $100 million lobbying for this plan because they are the ones that will be making *more* money. The legislation allows the drug industry to circumvent price control and avoid regulation. The consumer will see a $3.5 billion a year bump in drug prices.[8]

And the extra costs that they may face? No worries, they will just pass them on to government agencies, their own workforce and you the consumer. That is right; *you'll* be paying for this mess for years to come. Not only will the money come out of your wallet directly, but indirectly as well through the imposition of higher taxes that will be necessary to pay for it. And the shocking part of this—you will get little return on your investment.

You really think that the poor kids who live in Detroit

or Harlem are going to be the beneficiaries? I've got a bridge to sell you if you believe that one. Small businesses will really feel the implications of ObamaCare. They are going to have to pay huge payouts for healthcare that really won't benefit their employees. Small businesses will eventually feel the implications of ObamaCare. They are going to have to provide healthcare that is cost prohibitive and really won't benefit their employees. When small businesses can't afford government-mandated health insurance they'll simply just stop hiring. Or worse, they will lay off workers. Translation? ObamaCare means fewer jobs at a critical time for our economy.

Obama's policy initiatives are never ending, but even his proposal to push up minimum wage is a job killer and a surefire way to end hiring among small businesses. Entrepreneurs can't afford higher wages right now. Small businesses can't afford to pay more in an already squeezed marketplace. Once again, the administration is advancing policies that will backfire, slowing the economy's growth and setting itself up for failure.

Cap-and-trade is another great example of legislation that could have had a negative effect on the economy. The Environmental Protection Agency (EPA) defines cap-and-trade as "an environmental policy tool that delivers results with a mandatory cap on emissions while providing sources flexibility in how they comply. Successful cap-and-trade programs provide strict environmental accountability without inhibiting economic growth." If it sounds like a lot of garble to you, know that you are in good company.

In reality EPA's description of cap-and-trade is misleading at best and at worst dishonest. But no worries . . . Obama will have a plan B in mind following this failure too.

Even Obama admits his green initiatives are going to raise prices for electricity. On the campaign trail he said, "Under my plan of a cap and trade system electricity rates would necessarily skyrocket, even, you know regardless of what I say about whether coal is good or bad, because I'm capping greenhouse gases, coal powered plants, you know, natural gas, you name it. Whatever the plants were, whatever the industry was, they would have to retrofit their operations. That will cost money. They will pass that money on to consumers."[9]

You know what it really means? It means soaring energy costs, less disposable income, and fewer jobs in this country. Jobs under the Obama green plans and initiatives will head overseas to places like Saudi Arabia, where Alcoa and Dow Chemical are already setting up shop. Fewer jobs in the United States will ensure that Americans remain on the government plantation of dependency, subservient to foreign masters as well as their own.

Another irksome number on the Obama tally is the continuation of Wall Street bailouts initiated by President George W. Bush like TARP, the $700 billion bailout started under Bush and continued under Obama with the auto industry. Our bailout money didn't generate jobs for millions of Americans. Rather it went to wealthy bankers and their trader friends in order to ensure they could keep paying those elite golf club memberships.

STIRRING RACIAL TENSION

And if the economic policies of Obama aren't problematic enough, just look to the racial controversies that he has stirred up both directly and indirectly. During a press conference on health care, Obama was asked about the arrest of black Harvard professor Henry Louis Gates by a white police officer at his home. Obama veered off the health care topic and said the Cambridge police "acted stupidly."

Without having any of the details regarding the incident Obama weighed in on a local police matter suggesting the police action was racially motivated. He said, ". . . what I think we know separate and apart from this incident is that there's a long history in this country of African-Americans and Latinos being stopped by law enforcement disproportionately. That's just a fact." Once the dust had settled, Obama held the now-infamous beer summit at which Obama, Gates, Biden, and the responding Cambridge police Sergeant James Crowley met at the White House for a beer.

Obama's Department of Justice (DOJ) decision regarding the New Black Panther Party voter intimidation issue in Philadelphia during the 2008 presidential election also raised race-based concerns. The DOJ refused to bring charges of voter intimidation against the organization even with video evidence of New Black Panther members intimidating white voters at a polling location. The DOJ under Attorney General Eric Holder settled the voter intimidation case with an injunction against only one of the three members of the organization.[10] Following the decision, concerns were raised that under the Obama administration, charges of voter intimidation by blacks were not going to be aggressively pursued and this view was factored into the Justice Department's judgment in the case. That's what I call color-coded justice.

J. Christian Adams, a former Justice Department official who resigned over the case, said in a commentary published in the *Washington Times*, "I believe the dismissal of the Black Panther case was motivated by a lawless hostility toward equal enforcement of the law" and "Refusing to enforce the law equally means some citizens are protected by the law while others are left to be victimized, depending on their race. Core American principles of equality before the law and freedom from racial discrimination are at risk."

In addition, in his book, *Injustice: Exposing the Racial Agenda of the Obama Justice Department*, Adams explains how racial radicals have infiltrated the Department of Justice affecting the department's policies. The book reveals that while Obama was campaigning for president in 2007, he spoke at a New Black Panther Party rally in Selma, Alabama. Pictures of the event show Obama sharing the same podium with NBPP Chairman Malik Zulu Shabazz.[11]

Obama's silence when racial accusations were flying is part of the overall Obama irony. Does anyone who opposes Obama's policies get deemed racist? In truth, even I thought that we had finally put racism well behind us when the country elected a black president. Instead his administration is actually having a very negative impact on race relations by using race as both a shield and a weapon to defend his agenda. Now anyone who happens to disagree with Obama's policies is deemed racist. It's not the way it should be.

Conveniently, Michelle Obama's participation drew national attention at the NAACP 2010 convention. It was very timely. Was she invited simply to drum up press during the exact conference at which the organization had a resolution condemning racism within the Tea Party movement? And it's a little outrageous that Obama hasn't more harshly criticized Charles Rangel in the wake of tax issues in New York.

Interestingly Al Sharpton was on the scene to deal with the new legislation in Arizona that is being labeled racist for trying to control illegal immigration—Al Sharpton. According to Obama's friend, Harvard Law School professor Charles Ogletree, "Al Sharpton has become the lightning rod in moving Obama's agenda forward."[12] A front-page story in the *Washington Post* had a headline that read, "Activist Al Sharpton Takes on New Role as Administration Ally," suggesting a political alliance between the first "post racial-president" and race-baiting rebel rouser.

Why, early into his presidency, did Obama go off teleprompter and "go street" on the arrest of Harvard professor Henry Lewis Gates Jr.—a black educator arrested by a white police officer? Why even hold the ridiculous *beer summit*? How many people were laughing with me when they had to bring Joe Biden to the table to make sure that two savvy black educators weren't sitting side by side with one white cop? Why fuel the racial fires by getting involved at all? Don't get me wrong; I am not suggesting the arrest was fine or even legitimate. My point is, why is the president of the United States getting involved here? This is the guy that is responsible for appointing judges to the highest bench in the land. What happens when the executive branch starts interfering in the day-to-day operations of police departments? What happened to judicial independence? How many police officers are going to second-guess themselves before making an arrest because they fear the president will effectively label them racist for arresting someone who is black?

Part of the problem: Does President Obama even really have the shared historical understanding of racism in this country? Maybe that's the truest irony of this black leader's presidency. Author Dinesh D'Souza, in his book *The Roots of Obama's Rage*, points out that the president doesn't share the life experience of most Americans, let alone black Americans, as his upbringing was tremendously different. As such, D'Souza thinks Obama is more dangerous than many of us had originally imagined and that his presidency is potentially a conspiracy to equalize us with the rest of the world. Obama never talks about winning wars. He never talks about the oil. He seems to demonstrate a soft spot for resources in emerging markets, more than ours—like Brazil. We're not drilling here, but he's happy to help other nations drill.

D'Souza says that's because Obama wasn't raised in a place where the civil rights battles of the 1960s would have affected him, but instead was driven solely by an "anti-colonialist" and "inherited rage" against the West that comes from his African father.

D'Souza demonstrates a two-sided, two-faced Obama,

a clear Obama irony. The first being the face of an Obama wanting to get elected, the second being the anti-wealth, Wall Street–hating, federal regulation promoting Obama. In the book D'Souza isolates several quotes from a pre-elected Obama that ironically don't mesh with the elected Obama message. Take a look:

"We will need to remind ourselves, despite all our differences, just how much we share common hopes, common dreams, a bond that will not break."[13]

"A new kind of politics, one that can excavate and build upon those shared understandings that pull us together as Americans."[14]

Consider his words at the 2004 Democratic National Convention, which reinforces the notion as well: "There is not a liberal America and a conservative America; there is a United States of America. There is not a black America and a white America, a Latino America and an Asian America. . . . We are one people, all of us, pledging allegiance to the Stars and Stripes, all of us defending the United States of America."

And conservative themed words that Obama made on the campaign trail like ". . . the people I meet in small towns and big cities and diners and office parks—they don't expect government to solve all of their problems. Go into the collar counties around Chicago, and they'll tell you that they don't want their tax money wasted by a welfare agency or by the Pentagon. Go into any inner-city neighborhood to learn." D'Souza calls these quotes "inspirational" and words you'd normally hear at the "Republican convention."[15]

And where are those limited-government, liberty-touting

words now? Nowhere. This Obama is all about federal control. But even more worrisome than this shift in Obama's message, is the root of his anger. D'Souza makes the point in his book that Obama is an anticolonial thinker, with the desire to equalize America with the rest of the world, to put us on the same economic footing as the rest.

Perhaps Obama showed his true allegiance when he sent a bust of British Prime Minister Winston Churchill back to England. The bronze bust was a gift on loan from Great Britain to President George W. Bush. It was on display inside the Oval Office. And this isn't a surprise. For many of us, Churchill stands for freedom and victory over tyranny and evil. When the Brits told Obama he could keep it, he said no thanks and replaced it with one of Abraham Lincoln. What's the undercurrent of this move? It's pretty clear according to the British newspaper *Telegraph*:

> Churchill has less happy connotations for Mr. Obama than those American politicians who celebrate his wartime leadership. It was during Churchill's second premiership that Britain suppressed Kenya's Mau Mau rebellion. Among Kenyans allegedly tortured by colonial regime included one Hussein Onyango Obama, the President's grandfather.[16]

I suppose still waters run deep.

Since D'Souza is right and Obama's thoughts on anticolonialism are the very foundation for his ideology, we are heading down a very bad path. We are heading down the road to economic destruction at a far greater speed than maybe we'd thought. Couple that with the fact that Obama is creating increased racial tensions in the country and we have to stop and think why anyone would want Obama's leadership for another term.

I don't know how we calm the racial tensions Obama's created except to get him out of office. And we can't wait that long to start correcting his backward approach to the economy and job creation. To me, the fix seems so simple too. Lower taxes for starters and put the money in the hands of the people, who know what's best for their families. Americans know how to spend in order to provide what is needed in their households and small business, but big government is impeding the process. That's what's most frustrating.

Limited government in America could really bring about the change Obama called for during the election. Obama's progressive agenda is a disaster and will result in bigger government and less freedom. Our limited resources will be further constrained because the government will have all the power and control. We don't need higher priced energy in an economy that's already struggling, but that's what policies like climate change legislation and renewable energy mandates will provide. We need job creation. And we need working-class families to have more money in their weekly household budgets so they can spend and expand the economy and create jobs.

What's really maddening about it all is that Obama seems oblivious to the fact that we've been living in some pretty tough times since he took office. How many of us would like to be jetting off to Hawaii and Florida for multiple family vacations. Living large on the backs of taxpayers—is this the kind of change we expected from him? While Americans struggle just to feed their families, we watch the first lady vacationing in Spain with several friends and their daughters where she visited King Juan Carlos and Queen Sofia. Does she think she is a queen too? Yes, first ladies travel, but our nation is facing some seriously challenging economic times and flashy, taxpayer-funded world tours give the wrong message.

Home foreclosures are piling up and the jobless rate in this country has yet to rebound. Yet here we are watching television coverage of Obama playing eighteen holes with his friends, some reports say, *every* weekend since he was elected during his first year in office. He takes lavish vacations while a growing number of Americans are living out the staycation on the government plantation. And when they're not globetrotting, the Obamas entertained in the White House estimated to the tune of $9 or $10 million in 2009 alone. Despite failed policies and a declining economy, Michelle and Barack demonstrate an attitude of arrogance and elitism. They seem to act more like white elites than blacks struggling to keep their heads above water in these desperate times and that's wrong. And I get called a racist for raising these concerns?

Obama's radical policies are driving more Americans to the government plantation by using big business and elites (Hollywood and environmental activists) to help him. He will wheel and deal with businesses to co-opt their money, power, and influence so they use their resources to support his legislative goals. Unsuspecting CEOs have become Obama's useful idiots. If he can't get the entire progressive agenda (no public option for ObamaCare) he will settle for an incremental power grab and he or another progressive will get the rest of the agenda at a later time.

D'Souza is right about Obama's end game to lower our standard of living. And once everyone is on the government plantation they will get used to it, settle for it, and vote for the progressives who provide them with their daily needs. Already, almost half of the country does not pay federal income taxes. The elites will have *theirs*, and everyone else will be blocked from climbing the social economic ladder. Ironically, the policies the administration is peddling now would have prevented Obama from achieving his success.

We need change. We really do. Ironically we just can't afford the kind that Obama and the Washington elites are currently advocating.

THREE

Digging Deep Holes

It was the most memorable time of my life. It was a touching moment. Because I never thought this day would happen. I won't have to worry about putting gas in my car. I won't have to worry about paying my mortgage. You know, if I help him, he's going to help me.

—Obama campaign supporter, Florida Rally, 2008

I'm afraid that since that rally this Obama supporter has probably found out that you *do* have to worry about paying your mortgage. You *do* have to worry about putting gas in your car. Simply put the government cannot take care of the day-to-day lives of its people—we have to take care of ourselves. The government's proper role is to follow the Constitution and step aside so that individuals can take control of their lives. The Constitution is our country's blueprint that ensures liberty, allowing individuals to pursue their own path toward finding opportunities to improve their lives.

I have been reminded of the importance of self-reliance many times in my life. But one occasion really stands out in my mind. It significantly altered the way I think about the concept of government dependence. I learned that I have to function and survive on my own—nobody is going to do it for me.

I learned this lesson the hard way—my life was being threatened by a crazy ex-boyfriend. I had to get a restraining order issued against him because of the danger I was facing. I thought this meant the police would be there to help and protect me if I needed them—I was wrong.

In the 1990s, we had begun dating and eventually moved in together. We were living in Orange, New Jersey, and I was working in New York City. We met at a club one night and I really had thought it would work out. But the relationship fizzled out and I had to move into my own place. I tried to work things out nicely. I tried to keep it on a friendly basis, which was a big mistake. He wasn't going to let go and I had a big problem on my hands.

One morning when I was about to head out to work, he was standing at my door beyond the sight of the peephole. When I opened the door he jumped me pushing his way inside and we fought for about twenty minutes, which seemed like hours. It was rough and very physical. The fight moved from room to room as I tried to escape his grasps. It was really loud. Unless my neighbors had already left for work, everyone should have heard it—how could they not? Yet despite the noise, and my pleas for help, no one came to my assistance. No one came to my apartment. No one called the police. Looking back I confess that even I am surprised no one helped me.

I did everything I could to defend myself and not allow him to overpower me for one second. Somehow we ended up in the kitchen. Several kitchen chairs went down and even a few pots. I managed to get my hands on a baking pan and I struck his body anyplace I could and hard. He finally ran out of my apartment.

I had several bruises and I know for sure he did as well. My baking pan was no longer usable, and thank goodness for it. I missed a day of work to get myself together and just allow what had happened to sink in. I knew I had to take what happened to another level. Someone of authority must know about this. What if he were to attack me again? The next time one of us—or both of us—could end up dead? At this point, I had no idea what he would do. Come back with a weapon? Hire someone to harm me? So many things went through my mind. From that day on, I had a different perspective for women who were stalked and attacked by their "significant" others.

I went to my doctor and wasted no time getting a restraining order, because I thought it would make me safe. I thought it meant that I was being protected and that the police would be there in case of need. Clearly I was wrong.

It was a personal ordeal that dragged on for over a year. It was disruptive, upsetting, and financially challenging. I had to move three times. But nothing would deter him. He would show up at the train station or he'd be outside my church or in the lobby of my job in Manhattan. And it wasn't just me he would come after—he'd tamper with my car to make sure I always felt vulnerable even if he wasn't around. I felt so helpless despite the restraining order, because he was getting away with this. I was alone.

Eventually I realized that I was being stalked. The term sounds so cold and so harsh. It was hard to believe it applied to me. But there it was. These were the cards I was dealt in life. I was on my own. And I knew it. The government couldn't help me, and the police seemed less than interested in my plight. I say that all the time—you're on your own. But in situations like this, the point is really driven home to you.

There are a number of thoughts and emotions that arise when something like this happens. First, let me be frank, I never thought this could happen to me. I am a strong and capable woman. I thought that by alerting the police to my predicament, they would be there for me. I also assumed, incorrectly, that going to court and pleading my case would protect me. But when you really read the restraining order, unless the police witness the person threatening you, there is very little they can do.

Women across this country find themselves facing this kind of situation all of the time. I know that I was not somehow unique while facing this problem. Many women have sought restraining orders yet effectively remain exposed. Don't get me wrong, many police officers are very sympathetic. But really, their sympathy had no value for me. I needed help and it was not there.

This is the first time I'm discussing this event publicly

and I mention this deeply personal story here for a few reasons. I want to underscore that you have to take care of yourself. Don't rely on someone else to do it for you because odds are they won't be there. But second, and as significant, many people are under the impression that government authorities are the answer to all of our problems. But that is not what government is designed to do, nor should it be. The state is not intended to be involved in our individual lives. Bureaucrats cannot be our saviors. Government is there to protect our liberty allowing us to achieve our life's goals. In other words, the state exists to ensure our freedom and liberty—*not* to regulate our behavior, *not* to interfere in our day-to-day lives.

And remember, nothing is ever really secure and we should never assume it is, particularly if it involves the state. It is now widely recognized that many government pension plans are underfunded. This is happening especially at the local and state levels. It would have been better if you had put your own money away rather than handing it over to someone else to take care of it for you. You can't take out a balloon mortgage and think it will be okay because if you fall behind the government will help you. You can't spend every penny you earn and wait for the government to fund your golden years. You can't decide you don't need a job because you have welfare to pay your bills. We all need to be savvier about taking control of our destinies.

The bottom line is that you are on your own. Obama isn't going to pop by to deliver a food basket. You can't assume that Congress will provide you with housing or money just because you need it. If they give it they can take it away too! Take control of your life now; you are the only one responsible for it.

But what really troubles me about the black community is the belief that government is the answer to life's challenges. Decade after decade, year after year, the statistics in poor black communities keep sliding at a pace worse than other demographics in this country. And black leadership keeps slapping the old big government solution bandage on the problem; welfare, food stamps, minimum wage, and public schools instead of attacking the root or cause of the crisis. And yes, it is a *crisis*. President Obama and his warped policies are making it even worse too. Expanding government assistance, the love of unions, stimulus, being exempt from paying federal taxes, bad education initiatives, and ObamaCare will only dig us deeper into an already gaping hole.

WELFARE: DON'T HELP YOURSELF

Welfare has done more to harm blacks than it has to help them. But it's a safe place in politics—when politicians promise to take care of families with handouts, they get elected. The politicians can't always deliver on their promises and can't address the unfunded liabilities we incur through their massive spending, but those are secondary issues. Getting elected and in some cases lining their pockets—that is their first goal. Your vote is just a means to that end.

And like your friendly neighborhood drug dealer,

they've made you dependent on them. Not just financially, but psychologically as well. They give you enough just to let you get by, and live on subsistence, but never enough for you to get to raise yourself out of poverty. I fear that they don't want you to be successful because they don't really want you to get ahead in life. They have you exactly where they need you: relying on them for handouts each day just to get by.

And they want you to know that you can't make it on your own, that the system is stacked against you and that you need them to survive. Why would they give you the confidence in yourself to help you rise out of poverty? If that were to occur, you might be able to think on your own and question their tactics. By keeping you poor and telling you that you are a victim, they can be sure that when the next election comes, you will still be exactly where they need you to be. This emotional dependence on these self-serving politicians ensures that they will keep winning at the polls. Reliance is the only message that will guarantee reelection.

So let me make this clear: Welfare has consistently failed the black community.

Welfare tells us we can get money for doing nothing, and individuals with low self-esteem, poor work ethics, and lack of motivation expect the government to take care of them. Welfare was instrumental in destroying the black family. Welfare is an incentive for women to keep pumping out babies—no worries about the father, just get another one to keep those kids coming. Welfare tells us we don't need a dad in the home, because Uncle Sam will provide us with all the welfare we need. Lyndon Johnson's Great Society did great harm to black families, and welfare exacerbated the harm.

Welfare keeps the black community down. It has unintended consequences that hurt black families and keep them in poverty. Instead of helping the people the way it's meant to, it forces them to stay on what's turned into the "government plantation."

Tragically, there are people who need help. They are desperate. And some of the assistance is available through churches, family, and charities—organizations that don't bloat the government and set us back for decades to come. But truly rising out of poverty isn't done with a check from the government. If it could, we wouldn't need it any longer.

One fact is that marriage—not welfare—helps the black American family. The family unit is stronger—both financially and emotionally—if both the mother and father are in the home. Marriage consistently beats poverty, whereas government assistance entrenches dependency. In other words, government aid has contributed to the breakdown of the family.

Under welfare, women have children so that they can get that check for their survival. The numbers are quite staggering. The U.S. Census revealed that the poverty rate for single parents with children was 35.6 percent. For married couples with children it was just 6.4 percent. The chance of a child being raised in poverty if the parents are married and together is reduced by 80 percent. In 2009, this group of single parents got $300 billion in means-tested welfare aid.[1]

Consequently, black families have higher illegitimacy rates too, much higher than other groups. According to government data, 72.5 percent of black babies are born out of wedlock.[2] For Asians and Caucasians, those numbers shrink considerably: 17 percent for Asians and 29 percent for Caucasians. For Hispanics 53 percent are born to unwed mothers and for Native Americans 66 percent.[3]

There is a fundamental misconception about welfare. Many believe that the poor use welfare on a temporary basis just to fill in a gap until they can find work and bring themselves out of poverty. In this sense, welfare is viewed as a temporary measure for the downtrodden that need just a little bit of assistance to get back on their feet.

But the reality is something quite different. Welfare is not being used as a stopgap measure. Rather, many are staying on welfare like it is their job. They aren't using it to get back on their feet. Welfare has become a means to an end. And in these cases, it ensures that their communities are repressed and maintain high unemployment rates. These residents don't take care of their subsidized housing because they don't care about it. It doesn't belong to them.

This is the cycle of poverty. And it is astoundingly common among black families. That said, understand that I am not suggesting it's *just* black families that have become dependent on welfare. Welfare crosses the color line. But an unbelievable one third of the black community lives in this manner and such figures are not only consistent but also significantly higher than for whites or Asians. Blacks make up 12 percent of the population, but 33 percent of the welfare population.[4] If welfare and government assistance were so helpful, then that gap might in fact close. Instead it has widened. And why has it expanded— because of complacency among black leaders and black families.

Let's look at the poverty numbers in more detail. According to the Census Bureau in 2010, 46.2 million people or 15.1 percent of the U.S. population was living in poverty and the rate is up from 14.3 in 2009. And let's not fool ourselves. The addition of another 2.6 million people is a significant increase. Tragically, the poverty rate for blacks rose from 25 percent in 2009 to 27 percent in 2010. If we think we're heading in the right direction on fixing poverty in this country hear this: The number of people living in poverty in 2010 was the highest figure since the bureau has been reporting poverty rate numbers.[5, 6]

Very clearly, something isn't working. Still Obama is set to lock us into spending more on welfare with his record $10.3 trillion on entitlement programs to support the poor over the next ten years.[7] And guess what—that's not including the amount being tossed around for healthcare expenditures.[8] According to a report by the Heritage Foundation, President Obama will spend more on welfare in FY 2010 than President George W. Bush spent on the Iraq war in eight years. Adjusting for inflation, the money spent on welfare down the road will be double what it was under President Bill Clinton.

Clearly, Obama is the government plantation president. As long as we are getting handouts, we are going to be dependent on him and the other political elites who thrive on our inability to better ourselves.

Surely there is a better solution?

HISTORY OF WELFARE

Welfare in the United States began in the 1930s during the Great Depression. But in the sixties, following Great Society legislation, Americans who weren't elderly or disabled could collect a check from the government on which to live. Single mothers became the biggest users of the system. In general, it became so ingrained in the fabric of the nation that many view welfare as a right. In other words, there are people that think we have the right to life, liberty, the pursuit of happiness, *and hard cash from the political establishment.*

Many like-minded thinkers are clear: Welfare has negative, unintended consequences for the black community. A 1984 book called *Losing Ground*[9] by Charles Murray demonstrates that welfare has perverse unintended consequences for blacks. He argues that the system was created by elites with good intentions. They believed that the black population was discriminated against and that government aid would help to redress the wrongs. He said that the rationale behind the plan was that "the system"—not the individuals—was at fault. People could not get ahead in life because of the way in which the country had operated in the past. Murray's solution to the situation was, however, deemed impossible to execute: He wanted to abolish welfare altogether.[10] Critics chastised him.

But today, people are revisiting Murray's arguments and wondering if their original negative perceptions of the book were made in haste. Michael Barone, at the time a member of the *U.S. News* staff, is one such example. He notes that he is revisiting his initial inclinations that the book was "out of line with political reality." Barone now believes that *Losing Ground* "undermined the case that welfare was a moral obligation by showing that welfare created a moral disaster. It got people thinking that there must be another way. It inspired policy experimentation, which spawned political imitation. First in the states, and then nationally, welfare reform became one of the public policy success of the 1990s."[11]

Murray's more recent book, *In Our Hands: A Plan to Replace the Welfare State,*[12] published in 2006 suggests another plan, which is to stop filtering tax money through government bureaucracies and converting them into services. Rather, he argues that we should just hand every American adult a check for $10,000. So collect the money, pay everyone, and don't add restrictions, or watered-down services. Just the money. In a *Wall Street Journal* opinion piece he is pretty clear about the need for change. "This much is certain: The welfare state as we know it cannot survive."[13]

Look—maybe stimulus would have worked if Obama had just given the $787 billion to the people. Maybe a few thousand dollars per person and people would have been able to take some responsibility for themselves getting on their feet and back to work. Maybe we'd have dug ourselves out of soaring unemployment, record foreclosures, and diminished household budgets had we adopted Murray's plan or a version of it. Instead, the stimulus money got filtered through a faulty system, wasted, and spent. For all that red tape and bloated government—their commissions and their czars—did the money impact the lives of the people who needed it most? It doesn't appear to have helped or people would be working and able to afford their homes.

The problem with all forms of government entitlement programming is once the programs are established it's nearly politically impossible to end them. It's hard to stop feeding and entertaining the populous with bread and circuses once they become accustomed to them. It perpetuates the cycle of poverty and entrenches big government to administer it. This is the personal side of "too big to fail," with very perverse incentives. The antiwelfare thinkers are correct in saying that the welfare state is going to buckle under the strain. We can't meet the needs and expectations of people waiting for more and more handouts. The government has promised more than it can deliver.

HOW WAGE CONTROL KEEPS BLACK WORKERS DOWN

Walter Williams, a black economist, argues that the welfare state has "done to black Americans what slavery couldn't do, what Jim Crow couldn't do, what the harshest racism couldn't do." [14] The *Wall Street Journal* interviewed Williams in 2011 when his autobiography, *Up From the Projects*,[15] hit the shelves. Williams rightly maintained that racism isn't what has kept black communities from prospering:

> Today I doubt you could find any significant problem that blacks face that is caused by racial discrimination. The 70% illegitimacy rate is a devastating problem, but it doesn't have a damn thing to do with racism. The fact that in some areas black people are huddled in their homes at night, sometimes serving meals on the floor so they don't get hit by a stray bullet—that's not because the Klan is riding through the neighborhood.[16]

Williams argued that by setting minimum wage for groups like the youth and minorities, the government is actually generating higher unemployment numbers among minority teens. He pointed to the 1931 Davis-Bacon Act that requires higher wages on federally funded projects is effectively a racist venture on the part of lawmakers. According to Williams, the law keeps black workers off sites because most aren't in the union. It also ups the cost of government jobs, since the act also keeps the number of contractors eligible to bid lower than it would be without its existence.[17]

Williams underscored an important point: The socialist tendencies to intervene in the economy may or may not be based on the good intentions of lawmakers. Perhaps some have the misguided notion that they are helping the poor black families get by each week. But others understand that expanding the entitlement state and government dependency limits individual liberty keeping black Americans poor and subservient.

Noted black economist Thomas Sowell believes welfare is driven by social elites who want to impose their values and control the lives of others. Sowell says, "The welfare state is not really about the welfare of the masses. It is about the egos of the elites." According to Sowell, individuals engaging in the free market essentially eliminate the self-appointed role of elites to influence other peoples' lives. In other words keeping individuals on the welfare plantation is all about control![18]

Black men and women across this country can better themselves by helping themselves. Stop looking for handouts and protection from the government that is counterproductive to their long-term interests and well-being. Welfare, wage controls, and entitlement programs don't facilitate change. We do. We are the makers of our own destiny. We need to control our lives to move forward. Understand that getting government actors out of the privacy of our homes will ensure we all have a better future tomorrow.

Deneen Borelli

OBAMA REVERSING
COURSE ON WELFARE

In 1996, with a presidential election approaching, the GOP Congress forced President Bill Clinton to turn the welfare system in the country upside down with the Welfare Reform Act. Essentially, he handed welfare over to the states and gave each a flat rate based on population. In doing so, Clinton effectively downloaded the expensive entitlement programs to the state in the name of efficiency. It was a savvy political move because the popularity of free handouts barred him from dismantling them altogether. Instead, he just shifted the administrative burden and nexus of complaints to the local government.

Each state could implement its programs in accordance with its needs. There were a few central requirements, however, tied to the transfer of funds. The system linked some sort of employment search to the collection of welfare, rather than just an open-ended ability to live off of the government. There were provisions and funds set aside for the very neediest and caps placed on term of collection.

Here's how that all played out: The number of welfare recipients decreased by 60 percent. Sure, it varied state to state. But the bottom line was that millions left the government plantation and unemployment and child poverty dropped.[19] A study completed by the Congressional Budget Office in 2007 provided some insightful numbers. Families that dropped off the dole saw a boost in household income of a whopping 35 percent.

President Obama is systematically unwinding all of that effort as we speak. The numbers say it all. The stimulus bill will spend $800 billion on means-tested welfare over the next ten years. So get ready for this: It is going to cost $10,000 for each family paying income tax to provide $22,500 for every poor person in the country.[20]

In 2009, twenty-three of the thirty largest states, which make up almost 90 percent of the American population, have seen a jump in welfare cases, especially as unemployment benefits dry up.[21] An article by the *National Review Online* accounts for this reversal under the Obama administration:

Within 12 years, we saw dramatic results: 2.8 million Americans, well over half the national caseload, moved off the welfare rolls and into jobs. Many of them were single mothers. . . . Adjusting for inflation, total welfare spending has nearly doubled since 1996. In a major shortcoming, Congress reformed only one of the 70 means-tested welfare programs. And in the past two years, even the gains under TANF [Temporary Assistance for Needy Families program] came to a screeching halt. President Obama's economic "stimulus" package quietly created a $5 billion "emergency" fund. Bureaucrats used it to reward states where welfare rolls are growing again. Not even one in five of these "emergency" dollars goes directly to employment strategies.[22]

As the author of this article contends, once through the recession the government needs to reverse welfare spending and save $1.4 trillion in the process.[23]

Obama's approach to support those in need has backfired on the country. It has cost us more, it has not improved the lives of those most in need, and worst of all, it has effectively entrenched the poor to endure a substandard lifestyle. Times were tough before he arrived in the Oval Office—I am not that naive to think otherwise—but the failed stimulus plan has had widespread negative consequences on the day-to-day lives of the poor.

It's hard to accept that the first black president seems content to have us returning to the government plantation. Does he even understand that he is enslaving the poor to a life of dependency on handouts?

Just look at the statistics if you have any doubts. There are a record number of individuals actively participating in antipoverty programs across the country. In 2009, the number of welfare participants rose for the first time in fifteen years.[24] An astonishing one out of every six Americans relies on such assistance. In fact, a shocking 50 million Americans are receiving Medicaid.[25] The use of food stamps is soaring to levels never anticipated. According to a report published in Bloomberg news, the July 2010 levels of food stamp assistance reached an astonishing 41.8 million Americans. That constitutes one eighth of the American population.[26] Think about that number. There are 37 million people living in California, our most populous state.

Is this what "yes we can" was supposed to do for our country?

Mr. President, the answer is "No, no we can't continue on this path."

Yes, you are bankrupting the country.

No, you are not helping black Americans by giving them handouts but rather entrenching their jobless status.

Why are we still fighting this old welfare fight for the people in communities that should be helping themselves?

OBAMA INITIATIVES THAT HURT

There is a problem in our schools in poor neighborhoods. Black students are not finishing. The dropout rate for black students is twice as high as it is for white students. Data from the U.S. Department of Education demonstrates that in 2008, approximately 5 percent of white students left school while the figure for black students is twice that amount. That's right, almost 10 percent of all black students leave school before completing their education.[27]

Poor neighborhoods have schools that shouldn't be in business. Students are forced to attend the schools set out by their districting zones. Without a voucher system parents can't take control of their child's education and get them into a school of choice. This isn't going to change. Obama's children don't go to public schools within their zone. In fact, they attend private school, the youngest isn't even in the District of Columbia but was sent out of state to Maryland for her education.[28]

But Obama thinks throwing money at the education problem, with its untested and unproven initiatives, is the best approach. The stimulus package set aside a hefty $3.5 billion to help fix the existing mess. Plus Obama's lofty idea to dump $900 million into a spending program aimed at resolving the nation's high school dropout crisis. Obama wants to close bad schools, fire teachers that don't meet the standards, and address the way the schools are run. But, it's a large price tag for a program based on simply a hunch.[29]

Our students are failing and compared to the rest of the world, not ranking with their peers in any comparable manner. Still some states, like New York and New Jersey, spend about $15,000 a year educating students in the public system—a number far higher than that of higher-ranking nations. And for what? Their results are no better. Black children still receive a second-rate education because the political elites only know how to throw money at the problem rather than letting the moms and dads of America have choices and take care of it themselves.

Buried deep in a spending bill, the Democrats killed a popular voucher program for education, potentially keeping thousands of kids back into second-rate public systems instead of allowing for school choice.[30] In doing so, Congress stripped children of a basic need—a quality education that will equip them for a quality life. It is hard to understand how the country's highest elected official can endorse choice in education for his children, but not seek to advance the same opportunity for everyone else's children. Of course, challenging fellow Democrats and the power and money of the teacher's union would require putting children ahead of politics and that's a line President Obama will not cross.

MAKING MORTGAGES
A RACIAL ISSUE

Even buying a home has become an example of government overreach. The mortgage crisis that began around 2007 was very much a result of the American Dream on steroids. The message was pretty simple: Don't waste your time, if you can't pay the prime. But nobody was listening and the government thought everyone poor or otherwise had a right to own a home, regardless of credit scores, income levels, or the basic ability to understand a contract.[31]

Mortgage brokers took advantage of very low rates to draw in first-time buyers, naive about the housing market, and unaware of the terms of a low-rate draw that is going to grow after a year or more. Even those who owned homes, jumped in to load up on second homes, rental properties, boats. Many more just used their mortgages as bank accounts—drawing cash to buy things just because they could. But the highs quickly became lows and home owners and lenders became embroiled in a nightmare scenario: Payments became unaffordable and foreclosures inevitable.

Oh and what do the liberal activists say? The government must intervene and bail out people who overspent, mismanaged, and didn't understand. They used the crisis to stoke class warfare, ignoring blatantly that people should be responsible for their poor decisions. And yes, then along came the race card.

Jesse Jackson and his Rainbow-PUSH coalition, the NAACP and the National Training and Information Center (NTIC) jumped right into the crisis, using it to advance their political agenda. Masters of the victimization game, they blamed failing mortgage loans on the financial industry, saying that lenders took advantage of hapless home-buying victims.

These groups, among others, marched on Wall Street to proclaim this message, and the NTIC's *Save the American Dream* coalition sent a barrage of letters to investment banks: Bear Stearns, Morgan Stanley, Lehman Brothers, Merrill Lynch, and Goldman Sachs—demanding executives "pledge this year's bonuses to a national foreclosure prevention fund that will provide immediate relief to home owners in danger of foreclosure. . . ."[32] But the match up pitting lenders against the borrowers was only part of the strategy used by leftists during this mortgage meltdown. They screamed for full-blown intervention, creating new programs and committees and red tape.

The Center for American Progress, headed by former Clinton administration chief of staff John Podesta, proposed that the government establish yet another agency, to be called the Family Foreclosure Rescue Corporation, that would purchase existing nonperforming mortgages (at a discount!) with taxpayer money, offer mortgage holders corporate bonds, and issue new fixed-rate mortgages to borrowers in jeopardy. This measure appeared in several bills before Congress.[33]

One example of the proposed legislation seeks to grant bankruptcy judges authority to revise specific terms for troubled mortgages. Also under consideration is the Federal Housing Administration Modernization Act, which would allow the FHA to acquire subprime mortgages and offer fixed rates of approximately 6 percent. And then what happens? That's what's missing from these debates: a hard look at the consequences of government action. Here are just a few issues and concerns that no one is really thinking through:

- Allowing judges to rewrite mortgage contracts would add significant risk to lenders and would discourage new loans to those with lower incomes. Banks would be especially leery of granting new, potentially risky loans if the terms could be altered by a third party.

- The mortgage industry might further tighten its lending standards by increasing fees and surcharges and demanding higher credit scores and down payments.

- New homebuyers will have fewer opportunities to get financing on reasonable terms, negatively affecting the housing market and the economic recovery overall.

Foreclosure is never a desired outcome, but the mortgage crisis was not just about lenders taking advantage of borrowers. They fed off each other. Many people bought more than they could afford. While the American Dream was previously achieved through hard work and savings by putting real skin in the game, the interest-only loans and balloon rate mortgages allowed people to do an end run around the basic responsibility surrounding home ownership.

Personal responsibility is the key to fulfilling one's wants, needs, and independence. An understanding of the risks and rewards of contracts is the only way to avoid the temptation of overextending personal financial obligations.

Remember, we're the only ones who we can rely upon. Ourselves.

Frédéric Bastiat, the noted political theorist, wrote in *The Law*: "Man can live and satisfy his wants only by ceaseless labor; by the ceaseless application of his faculties to natural resources. This process is the origin of property."[34] Handing over this fundamental responsibility to the federal government would take us another step closer to statism.

IF YOU THINK IT'S SO GREAT . . .

Glenn Beck did a smart comparison on just exactly how progressive policies, like the ones Obama fosters, destroyed the city of Detroit. On a February 2011 show, Beck compared Detroit to Hiroshima.

Detroit, which was thriving and bustling at the time Hiroshima was bombed in 1945, is now a crumbled mess of a city with soaring poverty—double that of the United States as a whole. The city has been deserted by half its population, faces crippling unemployment and an education system that pumps out high school dropouts at the rate of 50 percent. The majority of students there qualify for lunch programs. It is the butt of national jokes. How many people move there by choice?

At the end of World War II, half of Hiroshima's population was killed. But initial government assistance followed by the drive and entrepreneurial spirit of a people, made Hiroshima what is now a bustling metropolis. It is at the heart of the Japanese economic engine with a thriving social and economic stature.

Detroit, as Beck explained, is the antithesis of the American Dream. It was created by fifty years of Democratic rule in a city plagued with corruption. Two mismanaged auto giants were not allowed to fail but instead have received government support in a variety of forms over the years—companies whose unions strangled not only their employers, but also their city. Auto union healthcare put American carmakers at a severe disadvantage. The cost of healthcare was passed on to the consumer, who paid about $750–$1,000 extra per car to cover UAW members' medical benefits. Japanese automakers' costs were one quarter of that.[35] The environmentalists didn't help either—pushing their green agendas for fuel-efficiency standards. The auto giants were forced to make cars they couldn't make a profit on to meet legislative, not consumer, needs.

And this is the direction we're heading in now with all that Obama is suggesting we embrace. Overspending, progressive government dole, and bailouts of companies that chose to be negligent with the way they conducted their operations. The Obama administration today is facilitating the progressive hijacking of the country and we're all going to be facing the perils of Detroit if we don't smarten up now.[36]

THE OBAMACARE RELIANCE

By design, this health care initiative exists to make more people dependent on the government. That's because Medicaid will expand under ObamaCare, which will drive more people to the plantation. Who will suffer? Well, that's a simple answer. You! Already struggling states will be on the hook for more taxes going to Medicaid. And who do you think will cover these expenses? You. In New York the cost of the state's $53 billion Medicaid program is partially funded through local property taxes. Financing Medicaid is one major reason property taxes in Westchester County, where I live, are among the highest in our country. Further expansion of Medicaid via ObamaCare will add to the tax burden in this state. Connect the dots: That means far-reaching consequences on the real estate market, which is already struggling.[37]

There will be about 16 million new users added to the government health care service. More people will be eligible because the government redefined the meaning of poverty. The Heritage Foundation in January 2011 wrote that roughly half of the anticipated gains will come from Medicaid and states will bear that burden. That may be okay for some of the richer states, but what's Michigan going to do? Extra taxes on those Detroit residents?

Any advantages of access to health care will be more than offset by the whopping dependence we are creating. Would George Washington or John Adams ever have imagined that when Americans needed medical care, they would go to the government for it? When did health care become a right in this country—at the expense of economic sense?

It is funny how Obama came to secure health care at all, while Hillary Clinton, during her husband's administration, could not. She couldn't do it because she lost to Big Pharma and other industries that mobilized to stop her health care initiative. But Obama neutralized the drug companies by getting cozy with big business in backroom negotiations. He turned to the drug companies to save his health care proposal, and just like other industries and interest groups, they aggressively lobbied for their own political agenda. Obama made the pharmaceutical companies proponents, not antagonists. He completely tilted the special interest power structure in DC by transforming potential antagonists to lobbyist for his cause.

The result: more handouts expanding the number of those on the government plantation.

Obama's failed stimulus plan has put our country in a devastating economic negative cycle. The expanding welfare state reduces the federal tax revenue, which leads to an exploding budget that places additional tax burden on those paying the bills—hardworking Americans and the private sector.

High tax rates on those footing the bill become a disincentive to work hard and innovate. And those are the factors needed to grow the economy.

FOUR

How Black Leaders Fail Us

Brown versus the Board of Education is no longer the white person's problem. We've got to take the neighborhood back. We've got to go in there. Just forget telling your child to go to the Peace Corps. It's right around the corner. It's standing on the corner. It can't speak English. It doesn't want to speak English. I can't even talk the way these people talk: "Why you ain't where you is go ra?" I don't know who these people are. And I blamed the kid until I heard the mother talk. Then I heard the father talk. This is all in the house. . . . Where did these people get the idea that they're moving ahead on this. Well, they know they're not; they're just hanging out in the same place, five or six generations sitting in the projects when you're just supposed to stay there long enough to get a job and move out.

—Bill Cosby, *Address to the NAACP on the 50th Anniversary of* Brown v. Board of Education, *2004*[1]

Somebody had to say it. And it was Bill Cosby. It was a deep and profound commentary on the black community taking responsibility for their families and lives. His concern wasn't about being politically correct. Rather, he was commenting on the deterioration of the black family, and teens. He took considerable heat from friends and foes alike for his comments. He faced a public backlash because he effectively said that good dads make their children's lives better and that fathers need to step up to the plate.

It is a sad commentary on our society that speaking the truth can be so challenging. It was a statement that many had been afraid to make. And it shouldn't have to be that way. A white person would never be able to express him or herself in this way even if it was from the heart because it would be dismissed as discriminatory. He would be labeled as antiblack for even raising the issue. And a black man, even one with the stature of Bill Cosby, was criticized as effectively being a traitor to his own people. Somehow people thought that if Cosby remained quiet, if we kept our dirty little secrets in the closet, life would somehow be better for the black community.

Seriously, is this the way we solve our problems? Cosby's commentary on the need for the family unit, education, and employment is a no-brainer. How could it be that someone like him could be so harshly criticized because he took such a commonsense approach to the ups and downs of daily life? Would those critics rather have heard him say, "Hey it's okay that black children are often raised by their mothers alone"? Or that "male role models really have no effect"? I'm glad that Bill Cosby set the record straight and challenged the politically correct community that polices our speech. I wish more people spoke up.

I think the language and behavior of young black children and teens today is very concerning. But for them and for society as a whole, it is very sad. There has been a steady erosion of basic language communication skills. The way you hear these children speak is not proper English, and the slang that is used will certainly not help them get a job in the future.

You hear it everywhere too. Have you listened to rap music over the past ten years? It's violent, disrespectful, and full of vulgar language. But it's not just in music; it's because of music videos, computer games, television, and the movies that this generation is not learning basic social skills.

And none of the traditional black leaders are doing anything meaningful about it. Not at school, not at home, not among leadership. Have you ridden a city subway lately and listened to gaggles of teens dropping the F-bomb and using the N-word? If you dare suggest someone curb his offensive language or improve his pronunciation, you are labeled a racist. As if the English language and race were somehow reflective of one another. Isn't that ridiculous?

As we know, first impressions are lasting and people are not only judged by their looks but also by the first words that come out of their mouths. Basic communication skills are necessary to get ahead. One needs to be able to express oneself in almost any job. Bill Cosby wasn't just talking about improving our use of the English language; he was talking about the betterment of a community. It would be tragic if an individual had great potential but was being held back because no one wanted to hire a receptionist who couldn't form a proper sentence.

You'd think the education system would help stop this slide into oblivion. But frankly, it's contributing to the problem. This is especially true in urban communities, where failing public schools are not providing the basics of reading and writing.

RiShawn Biddle is the editor of *Dropout Nation.* In 2010, he wrote about the deterioration of our children's reading levels and the impact it has on their lives. Literacy in the country is a huge problem—53 percent of black fourth graders haven't developed age-appropriate reading skills. They test below basic proficiency. In this country, 1.3 million students drop out of school and 6 million more just sit in special education classes not advancing—the percentage of boys is greater than that of girls without reading skills.[2] And you know what happens when children can't read: They end up in those special education classes that aren't helping and they develop long-term disciplinary problems.

Having served as a board member with the Opportunity Charter School in Harlem, New York, I'm well aware of cases where students are labeled as "special needs" by the public school. The truth is most of them are not special needs students but simply students who never learned how to read.

If students can't read, they don't graduate. They don't

get jobs. They have low self-esteem and sometimes end up on the wrong side of the law because of it.

Part of the reason the cycle continues is that children need help at home to get started in reading. They need encouragement and support. They need to understand it is more important than the video games their friends play after school. But in impoverished single-parent households, sometimes the parent can't read or is working two or three jobs and are not present to make learning a priority. Couple that with the fact that some teachers in this country are subpar and not prepared for classroom work, and you understand why we are facing this crisis.

Previous federal administrations have tried to address the literacy rates—but even the most recent, George W. Bush's No Child Left Behind Act of 2001, didn't make a meaningful impact. Most national programs fail to stick. Obama is approaching the problem by spending $100 million in grants to research why teachers can't get through to their students and improve reading skills.[3] A $100 million grant to study why teachers are failing black Americans? How about $100 million for mentors and teachers? This is the typical big government approach to public education that Obama and his administration have endorsed. Don't resolve a problem. Throw money, lots of money, at it. Then you can say you are working on it without having to really do anything about it.

Outside the classroom and the home, there's another negative influence. I understand that technology has come into our lives like a storm and that some children learn to turn on a computer before they even learn to write. But this culture of texting and Tweeting is crushing our children's minds: C U LTR. BRB. LOL. That's not language. And many of them don't see the difference. Using "U R" instead of "you are" seems commonplace to many. Our students think this is appropriate and they now use it when communicating with others. And you see it everywhere: on their school assignments, in their communications with employers.

And now we have some people suggesting we embrace this and just get rid of cursive handwriting all together. How can that be a positive move for these already language-challenged children who aren't getting encouraged at home or school? Many employers and lots of organizations still communicate with cursive writing—not texting. Explain to me how an office could hire a student who can only read noncursive writing?

A parent website called parentdish.com did a report quoting teachers who explained that cursive is a tool that helps children learn to read and communicate. The problem is that these children, who would normally be learning as early as third or fourth grade how to read and write cursive, don't even recognize it because they're programmed to read block letters on computers. The long-term implications of speaking in condensed text can't be good. There needs to be more discussion in this area.[4]

Worse, I believe, was the big controversy when Oakland, California, pushed for Ebonics in schools in the mid-1990s. A resolution was passed there to allow it to be used in the classroom as a tool. Ebonics is what's mostly referred to as the black vernacular. There are proponents suggesting that speaking and teaching children in the "native tongue" would actually help them learn. Can you believe that? What are they suggesting—that Ebonics is a language? Which employer is going to let them use it to meet with clients? Ebonics is a kind of slang, broken English that is not only tolerated among educators, but also suggested that it be used as an accepted form of language. In Oakland, California, in 2008, educators went so far as to propose Ebonics be used as a second language.[5]

I agree with Bill Cosby that parents and educators shouldn't allow the deterioration of language. How can children prepare themselves for a life outside of their poor neighborhoods and poorly run public schools if they can't even string a sentence together?

And whom can we hold accountable for this?

Clearly there's a lot of blame to go around. President Obama has inherited this mess after decades of decline. However, with a background as a community activist in Chicago, he should have been personally aware of the failed consequences of big government policies to solve the multitude of problems facing inner-city blacks. His efforts are only going to perpetuate the ongoing tragedy. Why work hard in school? The government will take care of you, feed you through food stamps, and give you free health care. Instead of promoting policies to encourage personal responsibility and independence, Obama's policies will sadly drive more Americans to the government plantation.

The lack of language skills, second-rate education,

and poor parenting are creating an environment whereby young adults lack respect for others. And they don't care about their behavior—they do what they want, there are no consequences. Contributing to this attitude are the online videos that go viral involving young black men and women, of a fight or individuals being verbally disrespectful to someone. Life cannot be about what is captured on those videos. They don't give context or background. Young children see these images and think this behavior is somehow normal or acceptable. It just is not the case.

Two powerful examples come to mind: The first took place at a McDonald's in Maryland in April 2011. A fourteen-year-old girl and her eighteen-year-old friend allegedly targeted a twenty-two-year-old transgendered person and inflicted an unwatchable beating. The only person who made an attempt to stop the madness was an elderly lady while a McDonald's employee took the video. By the time the police responded, the victim was in the midst of what appeared to be a seizure. What would trigger such animalistic behavior—by girls, no less? What kind of upbringing results in this kind of behavior? What messages are they getting that suggest to them this behavior is okay and they will not suffer any consequences? Their actions will cost them as charges were filed.[6]

Around the same time, there was a video that garnered national attention. It was of a fight on the New York City subway over spaghetti. It's difficult to tell exactly where or how the brawl began, but essentially two black teens are sitting across the aisle from a white woman. One of the teens is eating her lunch. Somewhere along the way, the woman asks "What kind of animal eats spaghetti on the train?" Clearly this is an offensive comment. But was it worth a fight? The altercation ended in fists and pushing, with other subway riders pleading with the young girls to stop and to just calm down. Thank goodness a black man stepped in to help the white woman or someone might have had to call an ambulance.[7]

On a personal level, I understand from my own experiences how problems at home can negatively affect a child's behavior and education. While I was growing up, my parents separated several times. As a result, I acted out with anger and frustration. I got in a few fights in middle school, I gave my teachers a hard time, and my grades suffered. But luckily I was disciplined at school *and* at home for my actions. I learned the hard way how not to behave.

Thank goodness I was able to turn my life around and not let the family issues drag me down. Unfortunately, today, far too many children don't get the tough love that I needed and received.

My outbursts were nothing like what we are witnessing today.

Sadly, the world has changed. What we're seeing now is a rudderless group of kids coming out of these poor communities with little leadership. There seem to be no mentors or people to guide them. Where are the role models? Where are the leaders for these black teens?

There is a significant lack of discipline in the home these days too, which is a major part of the problem. In a lot of broken homes, there are children raising children or even raising themselves, because they live in a single-parent household. The parent is working more than one job and there's no face time or interaction for the parent to really know what's going on with his or her children. This is part of the reason why so many disadvantaged children are not doing well in school—yes there are public schools that are failing our children but there's also, in many cases, no accountability on the parent's or child's part regarding discipline and responsibility.

Parents can't stay on the sidelines. They must get involved and *stay involved* on a regular basis. They need to be responsible and know where their children are, what they are doing and with whom they associate. It's the parents' responsibility to make sure the children are properly educated, disciplined and good citizens in their communities in order to prepare them for the future. Otherwise where are the children going to end up? The cycle of dependency will just continue.

Due to the lack of a nuclear family it is especially important for black children to have positive role models. We need more of them. And I don't mean a handful. I mean hundreds of thousands of members of the black community need to step up the plate. Oprah Winfrey is a great role model for black children—she has a real rags to riches story that can inspire and encourage the struggling youth. But speaking of Oprah: I firmly believe she should be leading the charge on issues such as school choice. Shouldn't she step up now with her time and money? It's good that Oprah built a school for girls in South Africa but what about giving back in the country that made her a billionaire? Chicago is on fire with flash mobs and crime. Why can't Oprah lead a surge of school choice reform? While money is important she has made significant donations to charter schools—but that is nothing compared to what Oprah could achieve if she put the power of her voice behind school choice. The $6 million she reportedly gave to charter schools is not nearly enough. Perhaps she is taking a passive role on school choice because she might face the wrath of the established liberal front groups, NAACP, teachers unions and alienate her close relationship with President Obama and other liberal friends. Taking a leadership role and the ensuing controversy might also cost her some of her followers and harm Oprah's business interests. Trust me I know the consequences of standing tall for liberty and I'm not a billionaire!

As I mentioned earlier, for years I volunteered for the Opportunity Charter School in Harlem serving on the Board of Trustees. I gave my time because I wanted to make a difference in this world. I don't just talk a good game of "Yes we can," rather I say, "Yes, I do." I saw firsthand the difference we made if we just gave children a chance—children who are already in an environment where they're set up for failure. These kids come from public schools that aren't meeting their needs. I volunteered my time because I wanted to help.

The school has very limited space because it shares space with a public school. There are hundreds of wait-listed kids who would really benefit from what the school offers because the education there is tailored to the child's needs. So if a child needs more attention in one area, he or she gets it. It's not formulaic—they're all taught on individual levels. The school starts at the sixth grade level. And sadly, there are kids who show up unable to read, because they're not learning in the public schools. It is hard for me to understand why the teachers, students, and parents are not accountable in some public schools. All the money that's been thrown at public education, yet we still have kids who can't read. Infusions of cash will not fix this broken system and the test scores are flat. You have kids coming in from low-income homes, whose parents can't afford private schools, and the public schools are failing to meet their needs.

I was at a fund-raising event in New York tapping private donors. We called it a "friend-raiser"—reaching out to individuals to introduce them to the school. I met a young man, who looked to be about sixteen and he really impressed me. He was enrolled in our school and he was a far cry from your typical teen. He'd never been to an event like this before and he was having a great time. It was cute to watch. The event was in a board member's home—a Park Avenue apartment—a part of town this kid had never seen. The size and grandeur of the home, and even the food being served, was completely foreign to him.

He told me about his days at school before coming to the charter school. He described his previous schools as noisy and full of kids that didn't listen. He said his routine now, which requires him to walk single file in the halls and in uniform, is completely different. He was really happy to be a part of this environment. He truly likes going to school now. And the great thing—he wants to go to college. I'm not convinced he'd have even thought about that had he stayed in the public school system. It was rewarding to see that this is what we can accomplish if we put our minds to it. Breaking this cycle of dependency can be done if we make a commitment to try new strategies and work hard at it.

In 2011, New York City lawmakers cut the city school budget by 3.42 percent or $271 million. But it isn't about the money as much as it is about how we use it. How do we best spend it? And here is the rub—we aren't making very good choices. In fact, we are making downright bad ones. As the New York *Daily News* reports, although these cuts were made "lawmakers also added $14.3 million in teacher pork for union-backed teacher centers."[8]

It's hard to understand the power of these unions and why they are interested more in protecting their overpaid and under-functioning staff than they are in protecting the students themselves. I'm aware of the challenges these kids face. Children shouldn't have to deal with this—no regular decent meals, no study facilities, and gang members approaching and hassling them. They come from single-parent homes and in many cases the parent works several jobs. Their reality is incarceration or the early death of loved ones. A tailored and caring school environment is the only chance these children have at a shot at a better life. Parents need choice despite what the NAACP says. This organization works together with (or is in the pocket of) the teachers' unions. In New York in 2010, the NAACP along with teachers' unions sued the city because nineteen failing schools were going to be shut down. The NAACP and the teachers' unions won and those failing schools remained open. They won and the bad schools survived.[9] The NAACP was at it again in 2011 suing to keep failing schools open. Who loses? The kids. Obama's girls certainly attend an elite school. Obama had a good education himself. *He* had the tools for success, but he's holding other parents hostage.

Bottom line: We should be using the voucher system, creating school choice, and creating online charter school options. We need to create competition, not complacency in the way schools are run. It's common sense. Monopolies are bad for consumers so it's reasonable that governments that run monopolies in education are also bad. With this type of system, there are few incentives for teachers to go above and beyond their basic duties to meet the needs of individual students and there's little accountability for failure.

A system absent of incentives works against both the teacher and the student. Competition brings out the entrepreneurial spirit and innovation in all fields. In the business world competition motivates and spurs innovation. In education competition would do the same. Importantly, increasing choice and competition have shown to increase student test scores across the nation.

So why is achieving competition in education so difficult?

Tragically, special-interest groups have rallied to block school choice efforts around the country. The teachers' unions that look out for the teachers (and not the students) want to promote their own interests. In some cases, groups like the NAACP lend their support for these unions.

Why would the NAACP want to restrict attempts to improve the education of hundreds of thousands of black children?

Union leaders want to maintain power and control. Their agenda is to reap in dues that are used to help elect progressive politicians. Once elected, the politicians return the favor by rewarding the unions with unsustainable benefits. It's a vicious cycle that bloats our budgets, raises our taxes, and keeps a stranglehold on the educational system. Union bosses are looking out for themselves and not the best interest of the children.

The NAACP, a once venerable group is now trying to paint the Tea Party movement as a racist movement. This is the same NAACP that beat back state-sponsored segregation in the landmark *Brown v. Board of Education* case heard at the United States Supreme Court in 1954. Once, the NAACP fought for equality. Now, the NAACP seems to be fighting to keep failing schools open and deny black children in low-income households an opportunity to obtain a quality education.

In Washington DC the NAACP, along with teacher unions, successfully lobbied the Senate to end the District's Opportunity Scholarship Program, a voucher-based system, initiated in 2003. It had awarded funding to approximately thirty-three hundred students to attend a school of their choice in order to improve their education. Although President Obama's daughters attend an elite school that will prepare them for a bright and successful future, Obama had no problem with denying educational opportunities for other black children.

To solve this educational emergency we need to take immediate steps to make a difference in children's lives to give them a chance to succeed. Every day we wait is another day we fail our children and our nation. There is no quick national fix. We need to do it locally, neighborhood by neighborhood, school by school. As Albert Einstein once said, "The definition of insanity is doing the same thing over and over again and expecting different results." Children and parents held hostage on educational choice need to be liberated. The cycle of dependency must be broken. The black community can no longer continue like this. It's time we break the insanity of government-run schools and move forward with school choice.

School choice will empower parents and free those children currently enslaved in failing public schools so that they can obtain the skills that are necessary to have a bright and successful future.

If the public school system worked, I wouldn't advocate a change. But it doesn't work. And we are being strangled by the teachers' unions to block change in order to promote their pension plans. Dropouts, reading levels, and the violence all tell me that this is a failed system that can't be fixed. We need to move on, and do it now.

There is some good news to report—the DC Opportunity Scholarship Program was a top priority for John Boehner when he became speaker of the U.S. House of Representatives and the House passed a bill initially authored by Boehner called the SOAR Act, reauthorizing the voucher program. In putting children first and not taking any chances, Boehner was successful in funding the voucher program via the 2011 budget.

How ironic that the white guy from Ohio had to press the first black president to give black kids in the District of Columbia real hope and change.

Here's what I demand of leaders with clout: Make an effort—especially when it comes to educating the children. Let's demand this not only of politicians. How about black icons in other parts of society—entertainment, sports, industry—why are they not standing up for school choice and other causes? We owe this to our future generation. If only Oprah would seize the moment and shake the shackles of liberal politics she could do more for the black community than the first black president. I urge successful blacks like Oprah to communicate to the black community how truly exceptional it is to be American. The free market system worked for her. Through hard work and perseverance she was able to transcend her humble beginnings and personal hardships into one of the most powerful and wealthy women in the world. She needs to encourage young blacks to follow her lead.

BLACK LEADERS, BAD POLITICS

Looking back at my voting record, I have to say that I voted for Democrats early on in my life, because my parents did. I thought a black woman in America was supposed to do so. I was influenced by the standard publications that the black community read at that time. It was always *Jet* and *Ebony* and there was an obvious slant to everything I read. There were always positive discussions about the left-leaning blacks like Jesse Jackson and Al Sharpton. That was the only exposure I had to black politicians too.

At around the age of twenty, I decided to move from my parents' home. It was time for me to grow up and start to take responsibility for myself. Before I left home, I worked two jobs—one for the Department of Motor Vehicles and one in retail at night. I started to really crave more in life than what my hometown offered. But I am not convinced everyone has that yearning because they are not exposed to what other opportunities are available to them. So they just stay and do what some of their relatives do and gloss over the standard black community material they are given.

I was the first person in my family to get a university degree. I moved away from the life I'd grown to know, away from the local traditions, and I learned a lot. I started reading different things. I was exposed to debates on public policy and alternative discussions. I really encourage young people to just read, step outside of the box that they have been locked into. Black families don't have to vote for black politicians or only Democrats. You can really open your heart and mind and hear and learn other ideas that are out there and worthwhile. There are leaders out there worth listening to and hearing and deciding for oneself if they're worth supporting. Status quo is not the answer. Just because someone is black doesn't mean they have your interest at heart.

It helped me too because once I was out there on my own, in a big world, I didn't fall back on any theory that I was owed anything at all. I never played the race card at my job. In contrast, look at Obama. He's the first to insinuate that the reason for the uprising in the Tea Party is to get the black president out of office.

A book out called *Family of Freedom: Presidents and African Americans in the White House* by Kenneth T. Walsh reveals a candid conversation with Obama about race in which Obama says he doesn't want to be thought of as a black president and that he is president to all people. He said he doesn't really think about his race, he has too many other things to think about.

But here is the contradiction. Obama does acknowledge race is an issue. Walsh writes:

In May 2010, [Obama] told guests at a private White House dinner that race was probably a key component in the rising opposition to his presidency from conservatives, especially right-wing activists in the anti-incumbent "Tea Party" movement that was then surging across the country. Many middle-class and working-class whites felt aggrieved and resentful that the federal government was helping other groups, including bankers, automakers, irresponsible people who had defaulted on their mortgages, and the poor, but wasn't helping them nearly enough, he said.

A guest suggested that when the Tea Party activists said they wanted to "take back" their country, their real motivation was to stir up anger and anxiety at having a black president, and Obama didn't dispute the idea. He agreed that there was a "subterranean agenda" in the anti-Obama movement—a racially biased one—that was unfortunate. But he sadly conceded that there was little he could do about it.

If race were really the motivation of the right, why would there be such a surge in black GOP members throwing their hats in the ring? According to the *New York Times*, in the 2010 midterm elections thirty-two black Republicans ran for Congress. This is the biggest surge since Reconstruction. In fact, a black Republican had not graced the house since 2003.[10] Indeed, I see this surge of black conservative politicians as a broader blacklash against President Obama.

Obama's solid support from the black community also started to slide around that time, as conservative candidates were speaking up and challenging his stranglehold on minority communities. Once holding a solid 95 percent approval rating, Obama's numbers started to slip. Before the surge against Obama, J. C. Watts of Oklahoma and Gary Franks from Connecticut were the only black Republicans to serve in the House of Representatives since the 1930s. Watts served in the House of Representatives from 1995 to 2003 and during his tenure he became the Republican Conference Chair—the fourth-highest-leadership position in the House. Franks was elected in 1990 and he served three terms.

But Obama's policies are so extreme it is no surprise that he awoke a whole new crowd of black politicians—even in the south:

- Herman Cain of Georgia made a splash on the national scene when he decided to run for president. Known for his role as CEO and president of the once faltering company Godfather's Pizza, which Cain pulled out of bankruptcy.

- Lieutenant Governor Jennifer Carroll of Florida represents the first black woman to hold this position, which she took starting in January 2011.

- California's Star Parker went from welfare mother to college graduate to 2010 candidate for the U.S. House of Representatives.

- Another southerner to join the scene is Angela McGlowan, who made a run in 2010 for a congressional seat.

- Princella Smith of Arkansas made that attempt as well in Arkansas's 1st District.

- Mia Love is the mayor of Saratoga Springs, Utah, and is the first black female mayor elected in that state. She is considering running for U.S. Congress.

And with sentiment shifting against Obama, in November 2010, for the first time in ten years, two black Republicans were elected to Congress—Florida's Allen West and South Carolina's Tim Scott.[11]

The political system really offers less political diversity among blacks. In the past, there was one answer. If you were black, you voted Democrat. No one seemed to care that the Democrats were enslaving the black population to a life of handouts and dependency. No one seemed to want to ask the tough questions. And it is very strange, as there seems to be a greater range of political opinions among white politicians. There are white socialists, moderates, and there are conservatives and libertarians. The black spectrum is very small. In fact, I attended a conservative event years ago—before I was a recognized public speaker. Some guy said to me, "What are you here for, the food?" It was in Manhattan—the high-society crowd, people with money. This guy didn't expect to see a black face in the crowd. That's one incident that really stuck out. So it is not just that black people think the black community should vote Democrat, white people seem to have this crazy notion too.

That lack of diversity among members of the black caucus creates many challenges in Washington. Congressman West, the only black Republican to join the Congressional Black Caucus (CBC), said the organization is failing the community it's supposed to represent:

> The Congressional Black Caucus cannot continue to be a monolithic voice that promotes these liberal social

welfare policies and programs that are failing in the Black community, that are preaching victimization and dependency, that's not the way that we should go . . . and those are not the types of principles that my mother and father raised me with in the inner city of Atlanta, Georgia.[12]

Republican Tim Scott declined joining the caucus because he thinks his parents would be appalled at the narrow-minded nature of the group.[13]

A CORRUPT CROWD

Sadly and somewhat ironically, if you judge the black community by its leadership, we are in serious trouble. It's not just what they are doing—promoting policies that hand out cash and benefits to keep everyone on the government plantation—it's how they use the system for themselves at a great opportunity cost to their constituents. The list of offenders reads like a who's who of the race-baiting, self-serving, politically correct crowd.

One of the most visible and hypocritical faces in the Democratic crowd is Democratic Congresswoman Maxine Waters of California. She's been a powerful force as lawmakers have scrambled to hang on to the minority vote in California. Consequently, she gets excused for not so respectable behavior. Famous for advocating the use of race to earn appointments for blacks and a constant rant that black Americans are historically disadvantaged and in need of special treatment, Waters crossed the line recently. She's always been shameless in her push for banks to loosen loan requirements for blacks, but recently she was charged after allegedly arranging a meeting between regulators and executives at a Boston based bank called OneUnited Bank. She was seeking to broker financial aid for the troubled bank. Guess what she forgot to mention? That her husband had ties to the bank and would therefore be affected financially to the tune of $350,000 if the bank were bailed out. She was charged by a House investigative panel, cited with ethics violations, all on the heels of her pal Charles Rangel's fall from grace.[14] Waters was charged with three counts of providing improper assistance, denied any wrongdoing and, like Rangel, sought an open trial before the ethics committee.

I'm not saying, by the way, that some white politicians aren't corrupt. They are. But collectively, there is a long list of lawbreakers whose communities really need their help. Their constituents' blind loyalty and no political competition keep them in power despite the miserable condition of their neighborhoods. While it's never acceptable for any elected official to abuse their power, it's somehow worse when the self-dealing comes at the expense of a low-income community.

ALL IN THE FAMILY

Michigan is one of those states that will struggle for a long time to climb out of the recession. It was hit hard. That's why Democratic Representative John Conyers's misuse of government funds in 2010 to put his son in a Cadillac Escalade was even more despicable. The taxpayers funded the car, but Conyers tried to sneak the money back into the kitty—waiting until Christmas Day in the hope it would go unnoticed in the news cycle. *The Hill* reported that Conyers wrote a check to the federal government for his son's car, which belonged to the Conyers congressional office.

"Conyers, the outgoing chairman of the House Judiciary Committee, said his son's use of the vehicle was inappropriate and pledged to reimburse the government." House members can pay for and use cars for business, but Conyers's son was using it for personal use, which is forbidden.[15] He was the subject of an ethics committee investigation for questionable use of office resources in 2006.

Conyers's wife, Monica, was given a thirty-seven-month sentence for bribery involving the city of Detroit. She accepted $60,000 in bribes from a company attempting city council influence.[16, 17] Conyers himself was again under the ethics microscope for writing a letter to the Environmental Protection Agency allegedly on behalf of his wife, who has financial ties to a businessman who would have benefited from a positive decision from the EPA.[18]

Louisiana has dealt with its share of corruption. Former U.S. Representative William Jefferson was convicted in

2007. The feds caught him with a two-year sting opera-tion. They used unmarked bills, to the tune of $90,000, which he stashed in his freezer. I guess it gives new mean-ing to the expression cold cash! He was charged in federal court with bribery, money laundering, wire fraud, and racketeering.[19]

Even when convicted, these guys play the much-over-used race card to explain away their poor choices. Maxine Waters did. She claimed the ethics committee was racially biased. Jefferson's advocates did too. The CBC cried *race* with regards to the federal investigation in which Jef-ferson was caught on tape taking a bribe. The CBC sug-gested a white congressman wouldn't have gotten any heat for getting caught on tape taking a $100,000 bribe. The CBC insinuated, even though the FBI found the cash in his freezer, that Jefferson was targeted because he was black.[20]

By using race to defend the indefensible, the CBC is showing its true color and it's not black. It's the color of arrogance, entitlement, and invincibility that is not race based but bred from years of not being held accountable for their actions.

TAKING OUR EYES OFF THE BALL

I also think black leaders are at fault for losing focus, which contributes, in my opinion, to the deterioration of an already struggling community.

There was a Pepsi commercial that came out right

around the beginning of 2011. Let me remind you of the environment at that time: The jobless rate was at around 10 percent. The economy hadn't recovered from 2007–08 recessionary times. Energy prices were creeping up. And yet, when there was an innocent enough Pepsi Max commercial, which showed a black woman flip out on her husband while they're sitting on a park bench when a white female jogger smiles and waves at the husband, black lawmakers sprang into action.

Never miss an opportunity to throw the race card to get some media attention must be the top play in the black congressional playbook. Representative Sheila Jackson Lee of Texas took on the ad with zeal, calling it "demeaning" on the House floor. She said the ad shouldn't have run during African American history month and that it was insulting to women. Was it really necessary to take on that issue? Is this what the elected officials should be involved in when the country is struggling to gain its economic footing? Weren't there more important issues for Representative Jackson Lee to get behind that more significantly represented her constituents?[21]

This next example is a little confusing, but let me explain it and you can form your own opinion. It's race-baiting gone awry. In 2009, when the Obama administration was handing out stimulus like it was candy, many Republican leaders stood up and tried to show fiscal conservatism. The then governors of Texas, Mississippi, Louisiana, and South Carolina were considering saying no to a chunk of the $787 billion up for grabs at the time. Representative James Clyburn of South Carolina held a press conference. Here's some of what he said about these four states:

> It's kind of interesting, because there's a colored thread that ran through that . . . the governor of Louisiana expressed opposition. Louisiana has the highest African-American population in the country. The governor of Mississippi expressed opposition. The governor of Texas and the governor of South Carolina— these four governors represent states that are in the proverbial black belt. That particularly insulted me.

Clyburn said he considered states refusing the stimulus money a slap in the face to African Americans, though he later backpedaled the slight to say it may not have been an intentional slap. In an interview he explained that the stimulus money was greater for poverty areas and that by turning it down, these governors were ignoring those who lived in the poorer areas.[22]

WE AREN'T LIVING IN KANSAS ANYMORE

Too many of us are living on the government plantation. Too many of us are living in poverty. Making matters worse, Obama is driving many more of us to a life of government dependence and servitude to legions of bureaucrat masters.

We will be trapped in never-ending poverty by the false promises of government security that sap us of independence, ensuring that the cycle of subservience continues. We have to take responsibility for ourselves and get ourselves out. Person by person we need to get out of the twenty-first-century cotton fields and integrate ourselves into modern society with independent thought and self-reliant action.

It would go a long way if we had some leadership to help us along the way. It would be nice if elected officials weren't spending so much time lining their own pockets. It would be nice if they made the black community a priority for reform rather than a justification for reelection.

But given the failure of black leadership in government, let's start to look elsewhere. Business, community, Hollywood, and sports have any number of black men and women that could step up to the plate and be leaders. Maybe they don't all support the Tea Party movement. Maybe they have other political leanings. But the black community needs new figures to step up to the plate and take leadership for helping today's black youth prepare for tomorrow's society. They can do it in schools, on the basketball court, or through their businesses. I am not saying black leaders all need to see the world exactly the same way. Rather I am saying that they can each make a difference in their own way. If these individuals would simply look at the tools they used to rise to the top of their respective field and apply those learnings to the broader black community, we could turn the corner and get on the path to social achievement and advancement. Imagine what change that could bring.

FIVE

The NAACP as Liberal Front Group

With regard to the initial media coverage of the resignation of USDA Official Shirley Sherrod, we have come to the conclusion we were snookered by Fox News and Tea Party Activist Andrew Breitbart into believing she had harmed white farmers because of racial bias.

—NAACP statement

Apparently, if you're black, but conservative, you shouldn't turn to the once-venerable civil rights organization, the NAACP, for help against discrimination. Apparently, this group helps only liberal-minded blacks.

Here's my letter dated July 27, 2010:

Mr. Hilary O. Shelton
Senior Vice President

NAACP
1156 15th NW, Suite 915
Washington, DC, 20005

Dear Mr. Shelton:

I thank you for your statement on the July 17 edition of *Geraldo at Large* that the NAACP will issue a statement condemning the use of racial and other slurs to denigrate me because I am an outspoken black female conservative.

I hope that the NAACP will extend this condemnation to all such slurs directed against black conservatives. From the family dinner table to the Fox News Channel, any black American faces potential denigration if they hold conservative beliefs. While I have grown a thick skin to the jibes and epithets, we all should declare that these often racist and sexist slurs have no rightful place in our nation's political debate. That is why I am so pleased that you extended the NAACP's support to help dissuade others from engaging in this grotesque behavior.

As you requested during our exchange on *Geraldo at Large,* I will list some of the more offensive comments over the past few years that single out members of Project 21 for abuse based on our race and our beliefs.

Allow me to note that these are not all just the taunts of random troublemakers. Take, for instance, a post from the popular web site of Oliver Willis, who works for Media Matters for America. In a February 10, 2009, attack on me and Project 21, Willis posted that I am "selling out black people while using my own race to do so" and that "black con[servative] punditry is a modern minstrel show."

In the April 8, 2010, edition of the Philadelphia Sunday Sun, a column by Wendell P. Simpson entitled "Project 21—House Negroes Stand Up for the Tea Partiers" states:

> *Project 21 wants to be the only Negro on the block. It defines its situation by its association with the so-called superior class. It is not embarrassed by it's [sic] status as token, and it does not rue its role as quisling. It is a willing concubine of the devil.*

While that just about says it all, e-mails sent to me and to Project 21 as well as comments posted on YouTube and elsewhere regularly call me and other Project 21 members "Uncle Tom," "Sambo," "house negro," "treasonous," "black tea-bagging ni**er," "sell out," "retarded," "hypocritical," "coon," "Stepin Fetchit," and a "modern day mammy," "descpicable [*sic*] piece of garbage," "black cancer" and "black bitch."

Here is one very personal attack on me that arrived via e-mail last weekend:

> *Please do something with your hair, every time I see you on TV you look like a NAPPY HEADED*

W__RE. You are an embarrassment to all black women. Please do not [let] Don Imus see you.
(petaud@verizon.net, July 17, 2010)

While something such as this might be laughed off, some e-mails are violent and threatening. For example:

I HOPE THE NEXT NOOSE WILL BE AROUND YOU ARE [sic] *ONE OF YOUR COLLEGES* [sic] *NEXCK AND HANGING FROM A TREE IN THE TOWN SQUARE.*
(alexas44@aol.com, November 19, 2007)

You faggot niggas need to be lynched by the Klan. I pray a nightrider strings you up every one of you no count good for nothing niggas, it would serve you right for trying to think that these crackers love you. I hate a house nigga worse than I do a Klansman. Rot in hell you scurvy doges. I would laugh to see your body strung up. It would save us real brothers the time and trouble to do it.
(qatazapk@bellsouth.net, November 24, 2007)

As we both seek a more civil debate, I am sure you are as appalled by these statements and the many others like them as I am. And I once again want to thank you for your on-air agreement on July 17 that the NAACP will specifically condemn the slurs made against me because I am an outspoken black conservative woman. We very much appreciate having the weight and prestige of the NAACP behind an effort to stop this unwarranted, unfair and uncivil treatment of people based solely on their political beliefs and skin color.

I look forward to seeing the NAACP's condemnation.

Sincerely,
Deneen Borelli
Fellow

Considering that when you go to the NAACP's website, the half-million-member-strong civil rights organization touts its hundred-year history by linking to accomplishments like the Anti-Lynching Bill and other milestones, it's a little strange I haven't heard a peep back on this letter, which among other things, threatens my public lynching.

But I'm not remotely surprised.

The NAACP has put aside the pretense that it is a civil rights organization and has exposed its real agenda as a left-wing promoter of all things progressive. The group isn't concerned about President Obama's race, it's concerned about his big-government policies and furthering them. So why do they ignore me? Because I stand in his way, and so they aren't going to step up to save me from life-threatening emails. What other reason could they have for not responding to my letter, which mentions attacks against me, my organization Project 21, and the very reason the NAACP was initiated originally?

I got a chance to confront Mr. Shelton myself before I wrote this letter. Not every black conservative has that opportunity. I speak for them, and I also worry for their safety. Here's what happened: I was scheduled to be on Fox News Channel to talk about the NAACP's resolution to condemn racism in the Tea Party. At its 101st annual convention in Kansas City, the group voted to condemn "racist elements and activities." [1]

In a release, the group used words like "bigoted" and "racial epithets" to describe Tea Party members. The NAACP claimed there had been a year of such degradation and cited an incident in which some claimed the Congressional Black Caucus were accosted and called the N-word.

Now, this incident, with the N-word, was never really proven. There is no videotape of it, there's no evidence it actually took place. That's why I was brought into Fox News to discuss this topic on the July 16, 2010, edition of *America's Newsroom*. When I was booked to do the show I was the only guest. But while I was sitting in the makeup chair a producer told me I was going to be debating Hilary Shelton, senior vice president of the NAACP, to whom I later wrote the letter.

I thought to myself: fine. I don't see myself getting an NAACP Image Award anytime soon. I'll debate Mr. Shelton. He just better bring his A-game because I'm ready for him.

So there we were live, having this debate. We were discussing signs with racial slurs and Shelton is, of course, chewing up the clock, talking in circles, filibustering, not addressing my request for audio and video proof for claims that the Tea Party members are in fact racists. He can't answer or address one single thing I'm saying, because he's got only one response: the race card. He can't tell me there is evidence, because none has surfaced. There's nothing that says this actually happened, just unfounded claims that get repeated and repeated. I wonder if his inability to address this proves he knows it's race-card politics.

I had a second chance to debate him on the July 17, 2010, edition of *Geraldo at Large*. This time Al Sharpton was along for the ride, arriving, by the way, fashionably late. I decided, in this debate, to turn things around and ask where the NAACP has been for me. Why isn't the NAACP concerned about my safety too?

He responded to me by saying, "Why, yes, ma'am . . . Just give us some details. . . . The very broad answer is . . . yes, we repudiate anybody calling you a bad name in the political arena." That's why I wrote the letter.

Like I said: not a word.

Let's look back at the history of black Americans. The NAACP originated to fight for civil rights. If you go to its website, you'll find many of their initiatives enacted almost a century ago, and they haven't done much to update their message: The Youth and College Division initiative: circa 1936. The Litigation initiative: circa 1909. Like you've heard me say before, update the message. One hundred years ago, even during the 1950s and 1960s, sure, we needed the NAACP. We were fighting for rights, still bearing the pain and agony of slavery. And if we do need the NAACP today, well then, they need to not be so choosy about who they claim to stand for. Do you tolerate hate mail directed at a conservative black American? Yes or no?

It's ironic that the NAACP has become a group of liberal apologists and progressive-agenda front men, because if you look at the history books, the Republican Party was founded to abolish slavery and then fought for a century to bring equal rights to blacks. Sadly, there are individuals and groups that seek to ignore and devalue our country's history: the history about slavery and the civil rights movement, to be specific. It is a widely held view that the right was pro-slavery and opposed to the civil rights movement. That's simply not true. The same tactics are being used today to misrepresent the Tea Party and make stick false claims that the Tea Party is composed of racists.

A book called *American History in Black & White*, written by David Barton, delves deeply into the true history of slavery and politics. The first slaves were brought to America in 1619. There's been some debate that when the Constitution was written in 1787, it was pro-slavery because of the "three-fifths clause," which said a slave was to be counted as three fifths of a person. So historians and thinkers of the time alike discussed the meaning of this clause. Why were blacks considered just three fifths of a person? Barton's Wallbuilders.com explains the reasoning:

While much progress was made by the Founders to end the institution of slavery, unfortunately what they began was not fully achieved until generations later. Yet, despite the strenuous effort of many Founders to recognize in practice that "all men are created equal," charges persist to the opposite. In fact, revisionists even claim that the Constitution demonstrates that the Founders considered one who was black to be only three-fifths of a person. This charge is yet another falsehood. The three-fifths clause was not a measurement of human worth; rather, it was an anti-slavery provision to limit the political power of slavery's proponents. By including only three-fifths of the total number of slaves in the congressional calculations, Southern States were actually being denied additional pro-slavery representatives in Congress.[2]

The self-taught scholar who escaped slavery, saved himself, and went on to be appointed to work in four presidencies—Frederick Douglass—was one such person who participated in the discussion. He originally believed the three-fifths law to be pro-slavery, but after researching it on his own discovered it was antislavery and, in fact, intended and demanded the abolishment of slavery. Here's why: He said it was meant to deal only with congressional representation to prevent Southern slave owners from using their property to increase seats in slave states. He deemed it had nothing to do with the presumed worth of the black man. This, from a hero among black historic figures.

So why do revisionists abuse and misrepresent the three-fifths clause? Professor Walter Williams says:

> Politicians, news media, college professors and leftists of other stripes are selling us lies and propaganda. To lay the groundwork for their increasingly successful attack on our Constitution, they must demean and criticize its authors. As Senator Joe Biden demonstrated during the Clarence Thomas hearings, the framers' ideas about natural law must be trivialized or they must be seen as racists.[3]

The Republican Party was founded in response to the Kansas-Nebraska Act, which expanded slavery to new westward territories, and the desire to return to the principles of freedom, and not see a return to rules that changed and encouraged slavery. It wasn't until the election in 1860, when Republican President Abraham Lincoln was elected, that fugitive slave laws were blasted. Democrats were fearful of how it was unfolding and so slaveholding states formed the Confederacy and took their states with them. Lincoln's election was the excuse by many to start the Civil War and modern defenders agree, but the real fight was by the Democrats and the desire for secession and the formation of their own slave nation.

Following the Civil War, the Republican Party advanced civil rights by passing the 1866 Civil Rights Act, which granted citizenship to blacks, the 1871 Civil Rights Act, which was passed to protect blacks from the Ku Klux Klan, and the 1875 Civil Rights Act, which stopped racial discrimination in public places such as restaurants and public transportation.

In 1883 the Supreme Court declared the 1875 Civil Rights Act unconstitutional, and it took decades before the next civil rights bill was passed in 1957 under Republican President Dwight Eisenhower.

The 1957 Civil Rights Act reignited the legislative effort to ensure blacks had equal rights that culminated in the 1964 Civil Rights Act and the 1965 Voting Rights Act. Pro-segregationist Democrat Senator Strom Thurmond tried to block the law by holding the longest filibuster in history—a record twenty-four hours, eighteen minutes.

Between the nineteenth and twentieth centuries, civil rights law advances in equality were stalled by the progressive movement. Led by President Woodrow Wilson, discriminatory policies were advanced.[4] Wilson, for example, supported segregation in federal departments and in the military.[5] Wilson's racially biased book, *A History of the American People*, was quoted in D. W. Griffith's silent film *The Birth of a Nation*, which was used as a recruiting tool for the Ku Klux Klan. Wilson showed the racist film in the White House.[6]

Wilson's views about race were a result of his southern upbringing. Historian Victoria Bissell Brown wrote, "To understand Woodrow Wilson's racial views, it is important to remember that he was a southerner. He had been raised in a climate in which it was presumed that African American people were less evolved than Anglo Saxon people."[7]

Democrat President Harry S. Truman started to reverse the segregation policies by creating the President's Committee on Civil Rights, and in 1948 he signed Executive Order 9981, which ended segregation in the United States Armed Forces.[8]

Eventually, the 1964 Civil Rights Act was passed under Democrat President Lyndon Johnson but the success of this legislation was due to the leadership of the Republican Senate Minority Leader Everett Dirksen (R-IL), who rallied enough support from his party to overcome the Senate filibuster led by Democrat Senator Robert Byrd (D-WV). President Johnson gave credit to Dirksen for helping the bill pass. Johnson said, "The Attorney General said that you were very helpful and did an excellent job. . . . I'll see that you get proper attention and credit."[9]

Of note, a greater percentage of Republicans voted for the 1964 Civil Rights Act than Democrats. In the House, 80 percent of the Republicans voted for its passage while 61 percent of Democrats supported it. In the Senate, 82 percent of Republicans voted to end the Democrat filibuster with support from 61 percent of the Democrats. Once the filibuster was ended the Senate passed the bill with the support of 82 percent of Republicans and 69 percent of Democrats.[10]

Of course, these hard-fought civil rights legislative victories were made possible only because of the heroic grassroots effort led by Dr. Martin Luther King, Jr. As we know, elected officials are much more likely to take a stand on controversial issues when they are emboldened by the actions of courageous individuals.

That's why Al Sharpton tries to conflate the civil rights issues with the concept of states' rights—using the argument often against the Tea Party. He tries to draw the analogy that today's call for states' rights by the Tea Party is similar or equivalent to the southern states' argument of states' rights to justify the Civil War. In Sharpton's world the federal government is needed to protect the right of blacks while power going to individual states poses a threat. Here are a few of the nuggets of confusion he has spun, according to Newsone.com.[11]

Civil rights are under fire and that the basis of the Tea Party is antithetical to civil rights.

Asked whether the Tea Party rallying cry "Take back our country" is code for "take back the country from its first black president," Sharpton replied curtly, "Take it back from whom to whom?"

If they (Tea Party) are advocating states' rights that's always been the enemy of civil rights.

Using states' rights as an argument in the twenty-first century is utterly ridiculous. To think that individual states would initiate any hostile actions against blacks or other minorities is insane. It wasn't until Lincoln's second term that the Civil War ended, and soon after Lincoln's death, so did slavery with the Thirteenth Amendment. The distorted understanding of history and the role the political parties had in the advancement of black Americans are revealing.

Which brings us back to the NAACP. Why has the NAACP evolved into nothing more than a front group for the progressives, liberal apologists, and victimization-screaming black leaders? They need to find some relevancy.

I think something worth mentioning right now about the NAACP is that not only does its leadership ignore conservatives, but they have actively paired themselves with many organizations that directly oppose the Tea Party—all, obviously, left-wing movements. The political slant is, frankly, offensive. The group should represent all black people. Instead, it has strong connections with liberal groups such as:

- Think Progress;

- Media Matters for America;

- Institute for Research and Education, which published "Tea Party Nationalism," a report denouncing the use of the slogan "take our country back" by Tea Party members. The organization forgot that both Howard Dean and Hillary Clinton have used the term in the past.

- New Left Media;

- TeaParty Tracker.Org, which was able to conclude
  racism from rallies with innocuous signs that
  said "socialism sucks." Is that racist? Guess who
  is behind this little gem along with the NAACP?
  Billionaire investor George Soros. So now the
  NAACP is on his plantation, keeping the race
  card alive by spending time searching for racial
  movements within the Tea Party.[12]

Clearly the NAACP isn't letting the Democrats do their
own dirty work. Why else would they denounce the Tea
Party, but not the New Black Panther Party, which intimidated voters outside a Philadelphia polling place during
the 2008 election.

Or how about ignoring racial slurs directed at black
U.S. Supreme Court Justice Clarence Thomas during a
protest outside a conservative gathering in Rancho Mirage,
California, early in 2011. When a reporter asked members of the crowd their thoughts on Thomas, he was given
quotes like "put him back in the field" and "string him
up"—all caught on camera. Where was the NAACP? Nowhere. The organization, approached by the *Daily Caller*
for comment, said only that they condemn all "vitriolic
language."[13]

It is fairly obvious what's going on here. The NAACP
is doing blacks a huge disservice. Leaders are standing by

idly when politics don't match their own. The NAACP should learn a lesson from the NPR incident that resulted in the resignation of NPR's president Ron Schiller. He leveled false allegations against the Tea Party and it cost him his job and a future job he had lined up. He called the movement "fanatical" and said during a discussion to donors, "The current Republican Party is not really the Republican Party, it's been hijacked by this group; that is, not just Islamophobic but really xenophobic. I mean, basically, they are, they believe in sort of white, middle American, gun toting—I mean, it's scary. They're seriously racist, racist people." [14]

Divisive, empty rhetoric like this should not be tolerated. Playing the race card is passé. Race-baiting and victimization messaging by the NAACP is unacceptable and insulting. Honestly, a look back at the history of the great black thinker Frederick Douglass should be evidence enough. He said, "Find out just what people will submit to, and you have found out the exact amount of injustice and wrong which will be imposed upon them; and these will continue till they are resisted with either words or blows, or with both. The limits of tyrants are prescribed by the endurance of those whom they oppress."

The Frederick Douglasses, not the Al Sharptons of the world, should be our role models. Once Douglass escaped slavery, instead of feeling sorry for himself or wallowing in self-pity or blaming the "white man," he became a self-educated social reformer and writer. He believed in individualism, liberty, and equal rights. He embodied three key successes in his life, which should be the mantra of all individuals and groups who want freedom. Douglass believed in himself, he took advantage of every opportunity, and he used the power of the spoken and written word to effect change—positive change for himself and society. Not cheap tricks, not manipulated language, not closed-minded race-baiting.

SIX

Green Liberal Lies

We can't drive our SUV's and eat as much as we want and keep our homes on 72 degrees at all times . . . and then just expect that other countries are going to say OK.

—Senator Barack Obama, May 16, 2008

Energy plans put forth by the Obama administration are nothing short of a conspiracy. Chastising gas-guzzling cars and the way in which we heat our homes isn't about the environment, it is about money. Plan A for the Obama administration to generate green money was cap-and-trade—an emissions tax that would have helped his friends in the business of new energy sources. The government actually had a lot of people duped on cap-and-trade. Newt Gingrich was even on board for doing a commercial with Nancy Pelosi. Obama's friend General

Electric's Jeff Immelt was getting excited about his investment in wind and solar, so he was on board too, but that didn't take much effort.

Before Obama took office, Immelt decided to make money on green initiatives despite resistance from both his senior team and his customers. Central to making money on GE's high-profile *ecomagination* campaign was making carbon-based energy—fossil fuels (coal, oil, and natural gas) more expensive via legislation. A law was needed to force higher energy prices and cap-and-trade legislation was the chosen scheme. Obama was the right man for GE and others looking to get rich on new revenues from the green plot. After all, he'd talked up energy during the campaign.

Cap-and-trade got very close to becoming law, but it wasn't because of the merits of the plan. It was simply due to the confluence of special-interest influence of big business, environmental activists, and progressive politicians in Congress and the administration. It was heavy-handed and manipulative and came close to working. But there is nothing free market about using legislation to create markets via taxing energy or mandating sales of products. Companies should profit and fail based on their business strategies, not on government backing and support. Period.

The proof of manipulation is in the words. Without laws in place and no new legislation GE can't make money—Immelt once said, "The only way we'll ever get a return on our investment in these technologies is if greenhouse gases have a monetary value." That's why Immelt and his venture capital pal John Doerr lobbied so hard for cap-and-trade. Immelt did not act alone: There was the

U.S. Climate Action Partnership too—a coalition of big-business and environmental groups that lobbied for cap-and-trade. Banks got in on the action too—they wanted cap-and-trade so they could trade carbon credits and offsets on an exchange. Goldman Sachs, for example, took a 10 percent piece of the Chicago Climate Exchange in 2006 and cashed out along with the other investors when its parent company, the Climate Exchange, was sold to the Intercontinental Exchange (ICE) for $600 million. The Chicago Carbon Exchange closed its carbon-trading effort in November 2010 after the Republicans took control of the House of Representatives. It recognized that the new power structure in Washington had eliminated any prospects of profiting from the cap-and-trade scheme. There must have been a lot of disappointment from the likes of Goldman Sachs since the carbon-trading market had been estimated to be in the trillion-dollar range.

The demise of mass-scale carbon trading happened just in time. If Wall Street firms could not manage the risk of mortgage securities, how could they handle trading carbon dioxide—a ubiquitous greenhouse gas whose only value is derived from government decree? Carbon dioxide is released from the burning of fossil fuels that currently provide 85 percent of our energy.[1, 2]

The Waxman-Markey cap-and-trade bill passed the House of Representatives in May 2009. Big business got a nod from Congressman Edward Markey himself for pushing the bill through. Fortunately, it went nowhere beyond that because it would have increased the cost of using fossil fuels (as per design) that currently provide the majority of our energy. But the bill would have mandated that 20 percent of our electricity come from renewable energy and greater energy efficiency, which would have been a boon to GE and anyone else who makes renewable energy products.

That's why in a company political-action committee letter to employees the moneymaking emphasis of Waxman-Markey was explained:

> On climate change . . . we were able to work closely with key authors of the Waxman-Markey climate and energy bill, recently passed by the House of Representatives. If this bill is enacted into law it would benefit many GE businesses.[3]

While cap-and-trade is dead—Obama and his allies will still push their renewable energy agenda any way they can. One strategy is for a national renewable energy mandate that requires a certain amount of electricity be generated from clean energy sources, but that option needs Congress, which with a Republican House will be a challenge. The other strategy is to drive fossil fuel prices higher by using the regulatory power of the executive branch to cut down on the supply of fossil fuels.

The plan is to cripple the coal industry and restrict the development of oil and natural gas resources by manipulating the free market system. Frustrate industry enough and they will give up on developing domestic fossil fuel resources—reducing supply is a great way to force traditional energy prices higher and make green options cost competitive.

Here's how it works with electricity. There are two technologies and one is cheaper. To advance yours (Obama and friends) you have to break the leg of the other one—coal. You have to artificially raise the price of coal in order to make it economically competitive with solar and wind. The EPA is providing a great tool to execute the president's plans. The agency is pulling out all the stops—using any regulation it can muster up to help prevent industry from getting mining permits by creating a regulatory environment that makes clear to utilities that coal is going to be very expensive to use in the future. Utilities will then plan on using other energy resources for electricity generation. Without construction of new coal-fired power plants, the playing field is opened for wind, solar, and other energy sources. Obama's war on coal is being enforced from the cradle to the grave. From making it harder to mine, from making it expensive to use, and by making it expensive to get rid of coal ash after it's burned. Here are some examples:

- EPA January 2011: Arch Coal had a permit revoked for a mine that was in operation. The EPA used the Clean Water Act to execute, in a rare step to cancel a permit already approved by the Army Corps of Engineers. Potential cost: 250 jobs and a $250 million investment. This was an unprecedented move that sent a shock wave through the coal industry. Why would an industry build a business when a government bureaucracy can walk in and shut down its operation? This arrogant display of power demonstrates the lengths government officials will go to meet their anti-coal agenda.

- The Sierra Club is on board and gearing up for a green fight. The environmental group is adding one hundred full-time jobs and the Environmental Defense Fund is hiring lawyers to battle coal. A Sierra Club representative said in a story in 2008 reported by the *Los Angeles Times* that their goal is simply to "clog up the system."[4] New York City Mayor Bloomberg added fuel to the anti-coal fire by donating $50 million from his foundation to the Sierra Club's Beyond Coal campaign.[5]

- Coal ash is also facing new regulations and it's still part of the battle. The left took steps to quash utilities' ability to use coal ash when the EPA deemed it hazardous waste and therefore fair game for stringent regulation and tightened oversight. Republicans, now better able to speak up on the issue, argue it has tremendous uses in building other commercial products.[6] The cost of calling this product hazardous? Well, jobs, for one—a study estimated that job losses could tally about 316,000. And then there is the cost—the price tag for the regulations could range between $23 billion up to $110 billion over twenty years.[7]

- The cumulative costs of EPA's rules are staggering. An analysis by National Economic Research Associates (NERA) for the American Coalition for Clean Coal Electricity reported the impact of the coal ash rule combined with several new regulations including the Utility Maximum Achievable Control Technology (MACT) and the Cross-State Air Pollution rules during the 2012–2020 time period was estimated to:

  - Cost the power industry $21 billion per year;

  - Cause an average loss of 183,000 jobs per year;

  - Increase electricity costs by double digits in many regions of the United States;

  - Cost consumers over $50 billion more for natural gas; and

  - Reduce the disposable income of the average American family by $270 a year.[8]

The EPA is also working on lowering greenhouse gas emissions through regulation. Through its endangerment finding the EPA grabbed authority to control the amount of greenhouse gases that can be released into the atmosphere. This will require companies to obtain permits for new and existing facilities. Facing the uncertain regulatory maze

and high costs to reduce emissions, utilities will
be forced to look for alternative sources of power,
otherwise no permits will be granted. The cost for
utilities is too high, so businesses aren't starting
new ones.[9]

Keep in mind that even according to the EPA, as
I mentioned earlier, the reductions in greenhouse gases
will have no meaningful impact on reducing global carbon
dioxide emissions. Gee, I thought we were trying to save
the planet?

The effect of Obama's war on coal:

- There was zero new construction of coal-fired
  power plants in 2009 and 2010.[10]

- American Electric Power, one of the country's
  largest power generators, said new pollution rules to
  address air emissions and coal ash would force the
  company to close coal-fired power plants and invest
  at least $6 billion to update its plants to meet the
  EPA's requirements.[11]

It seems the political, social, and business elite all decided to capitalize on global warming fears to work against
coal and oil drilling too. Sadly, their goal isn't to save

the world. Nope, their goal is simply to advance the progressive agenda and make money by being fearmongers. They're soaking the hardworking middle class with tales of global warming and the need for renewable energy, while the economic reality is just a transfer of wealth into the pockets of the likes of billionaires George Soros and Doerr (more to come on these characters), and a boost in the revenue of Immelt's GE, whom I'll get into more specifically below as well. In fact, Obama is even sending wealth to other countries, with encouragement and praise for drilling in Brazil while blocking it here in the Gulf of Mexico. It's somewhat hypocritical, no?[12]

Bottom line, we're rife with abundant natural resources for energy. The Congressional Research Service recently concluded we have more natural resources than any other country. But Obama is attacking the fossil fuel industry, especially coal, by manipulating the system to help his friends make cash. He's using any law or regulation that will shut down or halt operations and instead is pushing for the development of renewable energy sources at great expense.

The campaign by President Obama aided by environmental activists and his crony capitalist allies to slam the fossil fuel industry in order to force Americans to use renewable energy such as wind and solar power is nothing short of a conspiracy. It's a planned, deliberate, market-manipulating drive, not meant to save our planet, but to boost the bottom lines of crony capitalist corporations that use their political connections to rig government legislation and to subsidize their green initiatives in hopes of getting rich quick. Global warming scare tactics are meant only to generate profits and dupe the public into paying higher energy prices. Worse, executives have bought and paid for political help.

This scheme was orchestrated by Obama. It appeals to the animal instincts of his corporate political donors and the radical agenda of environmental activists allowing the president to achieve his anticolonial goals, while rewarding the profit motives of progressive billionaires. It's a win-win-win for the progressive movement. Crony capitalists make money, progressive politicians get a bigger government and more control, environmental activists lock up land by blocking development of our natural resources, and President Obama reduces the standard of living of hardworking Americans, bringing us in line with the rest of the world. Why should we care what the world thinks about the liberty of Americans driving SUVs or heating our homes to seventy-two degrees?

By lowering the standard of living of Americans, Obama is driving us to the plantation, and equalizing us with other countries and one another. It's a Karl Marx–esque approach to world order. And another thing: His climate initiative is just further evidence of his anticolonial views, which are in sympathy with those of progressive billionaires. I had to chuckle when I read Dinesh D'Souza's characterization of Obama and his relationship with his corporate pals in the insurance industry. He calls him "Big Daddy Obama" and says these guys are quite willing to team up with Obama as long as they "succumb to the government leash." We are getting the raw end of the deal.

A recent study by Dr. Roger Bezdek, a former Bureau of Economic Analysis researcher, showed that 2.5 million jobs would be lost by the time we reach 2030—lost to new rules surrounding none other than greenhouse gas emissions. That's right, the rich will get richer selling green products and the rest of us will see our household incomes plunge by $1,200 a year. Guess which group will get hit hardest and sooner? Blacks. That's right. Twenty percent more of the black community will be driven into poverty, and as soon as 2015, that group will have seen an income drop of $550 per year. In total by 2020, greenhouse gas emissions rules will have knocked out 1.7 million jobs for the black community.[13]

Also, EPA regulations, simply put, aren't about global warming at all—greenhouse gas regulations will have little impact on world temperatures. Scientists have said more than the EPA's 5 percent cut in emissions is needed to avoid climate dangers. The amount of reduction brought on by regulation is so tiny it can't even be measured on a ground-based thermometer.[14]

All the green talk is simply bad energy policy and *We the People* are footing the bill for this flawed green movement in a long list of ways. We're paying double or triple too—we're on the hook for Obama's clean energy stimulus, which contributed to the bulging debt, we will get dinged for taxes to pay for the debt, our tax dollars are subsidizing the implementation of renewable energy, and we're hit with high energy costs when renewable energy is used—all of which are taking a major bite out of our household budgets.

The additional cost of renewable energy is clear when you look at the amount of subsidies we pay per energy produced. Wind and solar power cost us $23 per megawatt hour and $24 per megawatt hour, respectively, while coal and natural gas cost us only 44 cents and 25 cents, respectively.[15]

We're financing the green initiatives through our tax dollars like it's a venture capital company, and Americans are the principal investors. But one thing: We're not the ones profiting. The return on our investment is that our money goes into someone else's pockets—some very rich pockets, in fact! A handful of wealthy liberals are manipulating the energy market at the expense of hardworking Americans. Taxpayers are not only paying to subsidize renewable energy development, but Americans are going to pay higher prices for energy, with added costs going to Obama's big-business allies like General Electric, Exelon, Duke Energy, and others that have built their business strategy on global warming fears. President Obama is aiding and abetting. The liberals who got President Obama elected are hypocrites and so is Obama, and their hypocrisy is costing the taxpayers money and economic liberty big-time. I guess we can't complain too much: Obama promised he'd make energy prices "skyrocket," and he has.[16]

Here's what's happening: Bureaucrats and big business are funneling hoards of cash and time into the next bubble—the green bubble—and guess what? It is about to burst. One high-profile example is the solar company

Solyndra. It received hundreds of millions of dollars from Obama's stimulus plan only to go bankrupt in 2011. Indeed, billionaire George Kaiser's family foundation was the largest shareholder in Solyndra and he fits the classic description of a crony capitalist. Kaiser was an Obama political donor and campaign bundler and he visited the White House three times shortly before Solyndra received the $535 million loan guarantee from the Department of Energy. Solyndra was not the only solar company to receive taxpayer money to go bankrupt, but is one high-profile example of wasted money.

And so, now the hardworking Americans and fixed- and low-income households will be footing the cleanup bill, just as they did in the housing bubble. Obama's big-business elites such as GE CEO Jeff Immelt and billionaire venture capitalist John Doerr will cash in and will be long gone and escape accountability for their role in inflating the bubble. There is a long list of these Obama green initiatives and some of them might sound to some really good on paper. But they are not good. They are simply based on self-interest, greed, and waste, to the tune of billions of dollars. Obama is the conspirator-in-chief, enacting policy that favors the bottom lines of those who have invested heavily in these green ambitions to seduce them to lobby for his agenda. Obama's big-business strategy worked with ObamaCare when Big Pharma lobbied for its passage and he is employing the same technique with his green energy initiative. Evidently, the message circulating in some corporate boardrooms is if you can't beat Obama's government, join it. To make money off of these early green investments, the administration and a few business cronies must work hard to campaign against natural resources here like coal in an effort to boost renewable energy resources like wind. With electricity generation renewable sources can't compete head to head with coal, so the cronies and Obama need to manipulate old-school pricing of cheap coal through government action to make it so expensive that the public and industry will be forced to use alternative sources to power their plants, their homes, and their businesses.

But Obama is only doing exactly what he said he'd do:

> We need to get behind this [green] innovation. And to help pay for it, I'm asking Congress to eliminate the billions in taxpayer dollars we currently give to oil companies. I don't know if you've noticed, but they're doing just fine on their own. So instead of subsidizing yesterday's energy, let's invest in tomorrow's.
>
> Now, clean energy breakthroughs will only translate into clean energy jobs if businesses know there will be a market for what they're selling. So tonight, I challenge you to join me in setting a new goal: by 2035, 80 percent of America's electricity will come from clean energy sources. Some folks want wind and solar.[17]

"Skyrocketing" prices, that was his goal, through one big green agenda item. Just another agenda pushed through at our expense.

STIMULUS GONE WRONG

Let's look at the manipulation of the stimulus package: $787 billion lobbied for like parasites by big business.

A line from an article in *Time* magazine best identifies Obama's real motivation for the stimulus package. "Some Republicans have called it an under-the-radar scramble to advance Obama's agenda." [18] In that same report *Time* magazine calls the Recovery Act "the most ambitious energy legislation in history, converting the Energy Department into the world's largest venture-capital fund. It's pouring $90 billion into clean energy, including unprecedented investments in a smart grid; energy efficiency; electric cars; renewable power from the sun, wind and earth; cleaner coal; advanced bio-fuels; and factories to manufacture green stuff in the U.S. The act will also triple the number of smart electric meters in our homes, quadruple the number of hybrids in the federal auto fleet and finance far-out energy research through a new government incubator modeled after the Pentagon agency that fathered the Internet." [19]

Let's look at how Obama's friends like Solyndra's Kaiser and GE's Immelt are making out in clean energy from the stimulus infusion:

- $2 billion to invest in solar companies;

- $2.4 billion toward electric transportation;

- $4.5 billion toward building smart grids;

- $5 billion dumped into the failed weatherization program;

- $3 billion toward jobs and innovation—claiming to create seven hundred thousand jobs by 2012.

Pretty good numbers if you're profiting from this green stuff.

There are claims that this investment will generate $150 billion in returns through related projects.[20] Hmmm . . . I don't think we've seen much of that yet. In fact, one documented colossal failure from this "stimulus" thus far has been the revival of the weatherization program. It's the $5 billion Obama dumped into trying to fix homes in need of energy adjustments, which of course the Congressional Black Caucus was strongly behind, because it promised training and jobs in the black community and promised to update the homes of lower-income, minority constituents through more government handouts. So far, it's shown only signs of mess, not success.

Here's what was supposed to happen: The $5 billion was to be used to infuse a decades-old program called the Energy Department's Weatherization Assistance Program. It was promised that it would create jobs and help reduce people's energy bills by updating their homes—sealing windows, fixing small energy-wasting items. Money was distributed to the states to be spent accordingly. Instead, the money was mismanaged and misspent, very few homes have been affected, and in some states, much of the money was used for corruptive behavior. The *New York Times* summarized the failure of the plan to deliver on its promises: "The weatherization program was initially delayed for seven months while the federal Department of Labor determined prevailing wage standards for the industry. Even after that issue was resolved, the program never really caught on." The story commented that Obama's promise to create five million green jobs over a decade was falling short of its goal and concluded, "the results so far suggest such numbers are a pipe dream." [21]

In Delaware, the program was such a debacle that it was suspended not long after it was enacted. The Delaware *News Journal* reported that a lot of money went to contractors who went into a home to seal up windows and insulate attics and instead milked the system by replacing furnaces, windows, and doors, while jacking up the price. Similar problems turned up in Florida, Illinois, New Jersey, Pennsylvania, Texas, Tennessee, and Virginia. [22]

Illinois didn't come up with great grades either. In late 2010 an audit was done on the state's weatherization program by the Department of Energy's inspector general. Illinois got $242 million of the $5 billion to put toward fixing a planned 27,000 homes. Many agencies were called up to distribute the funds, but the Community and Economic Development Association (CEDA) got a very large chunk—$91 million over three years for almost half of the total homes to be weatherized. But it seems, according to the report, this money wasn't being used to its fullest potential. Here are the phrases that were used to describe the few homes that did get fitted:

- substandard workmanship;

- improperly performed heating systems . . . (that) emit carbon monoxide at higher than acceptable levels;

- inappropriate weatherization measures and overlooked key measures;

- contractors billed for labor charges . . . not incurred;

- billing issues pervasive . . . 7 of 10 sampled were cited;

- wasteful material costs.

The main conclusion from this Illinois-specific report:

Our testing revealed substandard performance in weatherization workmanship, initial home assessments, and contractor billing. These problems were of such significance that they put the integrity of the entire Program at risk, although Illinois and CEDA asserted during the audit that they were in the process of improving performance.

Weatherization is not the only waste of tax money in the clean energy stimulus. An October 25, 2010, memo from Obama's senior advisors, including Larry Summers, Carol Browner, and Joe Biden's chief of staff Ron Klain, recommended that the president cut funding for the federal loan-guarantee program. Its goal was to encourage construction of renewable energy projects like wind and solar farms.

Obama's advisors singled out the Shepherds Flat wind project in Oregon as an example of an effort that was "double-dipping" because it was receiving multiple avenues of taxpayer support—in addition to the $300 million loan guarantee, the project was also getting $238 million in state aid, $500 million in federal grants, and $200 million in federal and state tax benefits.

They concluded, "The government would provide a significant subsidy (65+%), while the sponsor would provide little skin in the game (equity about 10%)." That's a great deal for the business interests but a lousy deal for us taxpayers. Oh, and guess who was one of the sponsors of the project—none other than the corporate parasite GE!![23]

In the end, however, politics dictated the day. Rather than admitting the failure of the loan program, which might have cast a negative light on the clean energy stimulus effort and anger congressional Democrats, Obama chose to keep the program: "The Administration is committed to the 1705 loan program and the role it plays in helping us bring about a clean energy economy and creating jobs in this burgeoning industry."[24]

We wouldn't want to antagonize powerful allies, now would we, even if it meant taking money out of the pockets of hardworking Americans?

SO, WHY NOT COAL?

If Obama and friends have their way, they'll wipe coal production off the map. It's obvious why Obama is so hyped up about clean energy—he wants to funnel government cash into the pockets of his cronies so they lobby for his anticolonialist progressive agenda. But why is he so set on doing it at the expense of an energy source that is cheap, provides good-paying jobs for 134,000 people[25] in our country, and is bountiful? Coal is the center of his target. Obama wants to steer us away from using it by breaking the industry's back. He wants it to collapse in order to force the use of the new energy resources. He's using every possible regulation to shut coal down, jack up prices, and drive money to renewable, green projects. He is making the industry suffer and ensuring prices rise to essentially mandate his clean energy future.

We have an abundance of coal. We are the Saudi Arabia of coal. In fact, about 45 percent of our electricity comes from coal.[26] Some states, such as Indiana where electricity is less expensive, get more than 90 percent of their power from coal. In states like New York that get only about 10 percent of power from coal, electricity prices are two times higher than in Indiana.[27]

A LITTLE TOO COZY ON
THE GREEN FRONT

So who are these billionaires and CEOs who stand to rake it in if this green agenda makes it?

First there is Jeff Immelt, the CEO of GE, whose company plans to invest $10 billion in environmentally friendly products by 2015 with a revenue goal of $20 billion a year by 2010.[28]

You know our country is in serious trouble when special interests rule the day. Immelt is the special-interest king. He has a poor track record running a corporation and this desperation led him to partner with Obama in believing the government is the answer to boosting GE's profits. GE lobbied hard for Obama's $787 billion stimulus plan and received tens of millions of dollars in government grants and contracts as a result.

Never mind the economic pain that will be felt by hardworking Americans from the Obama-Immelt scheme to raise the price of fossil fuels to make GE's renewable energy products more competitive and save Immelt's job.

During one weekly address in January 2011, Obama said Immelt is "one of the most imaginative and visionary business leaders in America."[29] But really, their relationship and Immelt's appointment to the economic recovery board aren't based on mutual respect. They're based on their common goal: pushing renewable energy.

Obama wants to build a "green economy" where energy is derived from renewable energy sources such as wind turbines and solar panels, while Immelt has a vested interest in selling GE's renewal energy technologies. He started down that road long before anybody knew Obama was seeking the Oval Office. GE is one of the largest producers of renewable energy products. Unfortunately, this connection proves very clearly that Obama and Immelt don't want the free market to decide the fate of renewable energy—they prefer the strong arm of government to mandate the use of alternative energy. That's why Immelt was one of the most aggressive supporters of Obama's cap-and-trade energy policy. The conflict of interest here is simply overwhelming. Immelt was a member of Obama's Economic Recovery Advisory Board, which was replaced by the new Council on Jobs and Competitiveness, and Immelt was appointed chairman. Immelt is also a frequent White House visitor and travel partner. Immelt even joined Obama on a recent trip to India. It's so blatant, their teaming up on energy. Even in the wake of the Solyndra bankruptcy, Obama's jobs panel interim report, "Taking Action, Building Confidence," makes five recommendations, including an initiative to "Invest Aggressively and Efficiently in Cutting-Edge Infrastructure and Energy," which calls for government support to improve the country's energy infrastructure and a new federal financing institution funded with $1 to $2 billion per year to amplify clean energy investments.

MORE BILLIONAIRES WITH BENEFITS

It's not just Immelt either. Obama is wasting political capital and gambling his political future on the likes of many billionaires and business leaders.

Billionaire investor George Soros and managing partner at the venture capital firm Kleiner Perkins Caufield & Byers John Doerr are two additional financiers whose pockets Obama is lining through these green initiatives.

Doerr, an internet-investing icon, placed a huge bet on renewable energy, but to cash in, he needs the perfect storm for fossil fuels. He needs prices to go up—cap-and-trade would have been nice for him. Now he needs the cradle-to-grave EPA regulations including a crackdown on greenhouse gas emissions to game the political system to his favor and as a backup mandate that the country use renewable energy. Apparently, Obama wants to help him achieve all of this.

Curiously, soaring gas prices impeding economic growth haven't boded well in previous election years for incumbents. The public doesn't warm up to losing that chunk of their monthly household budget to fill the tank of their cars. It's curious, then, with that palpable risk on the table, that President Obama is doubling down on his war on fossil fuels, making himself very vulnerable to criticism and even public outrage.

On the surface it seems like Obama is letting billionaires such as Soros, Kaiser, and Doerr with evident self-interest pull his anti–fossil fuel strings to ensure a payoff for their huge investments in renewable energy and the green economy. More likely, however, Obama is willing to lose an election to advance his anticolonial passion.

Tim Carney of the *Washington Examiner* wrote about how Soros in early 2011 announced a green investment fund to cash in on clean energy technology, banking on liberal politicians and their big-government funding for green technologies to ensure a return on his investment.[30] And it's not the first time he gambled big on green. In 2009, Soros pledged to invest $1 billion in clean energy technologies and an additional $100 million in the Climate Policy Initiative, an organization "whose mission is to assess, diagnose, and support nations' efforts to achieve low-carbon growth."

It's nothing short of bankrolling a return through public policy. As Glenn Beck reported in his *Crime Inc.* segment on Fox News Channel, Soros wants to get a return on his investments by leveraging his financial support for groups such as the Center for American Progress, groups that actively promote Obama's energy agenda. And Obama doesn't seem to mind being played one bit.

Obama's buddy billionaire Doerr is using the same strategy to line his pockets. He went long on renewable energy sources but he needs to bank on public policy to make a return. He was an early investor in companies like Amazon and Google, so he's reached the top of the venture capitalist ladder in Silicon Valley. But to reach the potential for green in a green bubble, Doerr and other investors like him are relentlessly securing their investments.

Ignoring free market capitalism, Doerr helped fund a

campaign to defeat a voter initiative to halt California's global warming law. He spent $2.1 million, in fact, to defeat the vote—called Proposition 23.

In addition to wanting to line his pockets even more, John Doerr has deep-seated progressive views and a clear distaste for the simple pleasures of everyday Americans. He apparently feels if left to their own choices, Americans in the flyover states will drive SUVs and—horror—drink bottled water from an exotic country. So those choices need to be eliminated through the force of government. The following are some of the elitist comments he made during a speech at the TED Conferences during March 7–10, 2007, in Monterey, California:[31]

- It does seem really hard to get consumers to do the right thing.

- It is stupid that we use two tons of steel, glass, and plastic to haul our sorry selves to the shopping mall.

- It's stupid that we put water in plastic bottles in Fiji and ship it here.

- It's hard to change consumer behavior because consumers don't know how much this stuff costs.

- Do you know, do you know how much CO_2 you generated to drive here or fly here?

But Doerr needed to team with the likes of Obama, because buying into green isn't like buying the usual high tech. Clean energy requires political advocacy to survive. The Achilles' heel of clean energy is that it can't compete with fossil fuels—coal, oil, and natural gas—on a cost basis. That means he needs the government on board to jack up energy prices before people will fall for the new stuff like wind and solar.

A case could even be made that as an original investor in Google, and current board member, Doerr is behind the green energy initiatives Google is supporting—$350 million worth! It used to be that board members represented the interests of shareholders. How old-school. Doerr's firm and Google have invested in the same renewable energy start-up company: AltaRock. This looks like a conflict of interest and also a possible violation of Google's code-of-conduct policy. The National Center for Public Policy Research, the nonprofit that I work for, filed a shareholder proposal in 2011 to investigate this matter further.

Doerr's company dumped $200 million into what they're calling "greentech"—the term refers to all things green. The thing with greentech is, it does not have inherited demand. Doerr needs to milk political capital before the green bubble bursts. So he's working with corporations and politicians he is supporting (reportedly he's donated $31 million to back candidates he deems useful).[32] Obama and Doerr are working with each other for their respective agendas.

EXELON

Exelon—Obama's energy company of choice—is another example of strange green and corporate bedfellows. Former Obama advisor David Axelrod was a consultant for Exelon. Newly elected mayor of Chicago and former White House chief of staff Rahm Emmanuel's biggest deal while working at the investment firm Wasserstein Perella was the merger that created Exelon. In two years at the firm, Emanuel made $16.2 million. Guess what happened shortly after the two companies became one? Well, they sold off most of the coal operations they held,[33] perhaps tipping its hand that the company was going to attack coal-fired power.

Not surprisingly, Exelon's executives were big donors for Obama's political career.

Like GE, Exelon bet big on cap-and-trade, trying to leverage its connections with the Obama administration. The company's large nuclear power generation would have given the company a huge cost advantage over coal-burning utilities since nuclear power does not produce carbon dioxide emissions. Exelon claimed that under one scenario of cap-and-trade the company could boost its revenue by $1.1 billion a year.

How important was cap-and-trade to Exelon?

According to stock analyst Angie Storozynski at Macquarie Capital Inc., "If carbon does not pass, it's not going to be pretty (for Exelon). . . . Unless you have some indication of carbon caps being imminent, the stock is not going to perform well."[34]

With dollars dancing in his head, Exelon CEO John Rowe pushed hard for cap-and-trade. It was reported that Emanuel asked Rowe to lobby for the bill the night before the Waxman-Markey cap-and-trade vote. An Exelon lobbyist boasted, "We are proud to be the President's utility."[35]

WHY NOT DRILLING?

The EPA's reach and crackdown extends to oil drilling: Shell had planned to drill for oil off the coast of Alaska in the Arctic Ocean, but the EPA has forced the oil giant to put the brakes on by not granting air rights permits.[36] The plan to proceed has been in place for years, and the company has invested $4 billion in planning already. At stake: 27 billion barrels of oil and an ability to keep production in this country and not drive it overseas. We're seeing a decline in production to the tune of 7 percent per year in Alaska. An additional problem is that a group of companies are paying for the cost of an existing pipeline. If you don't have enough material to pump through the pipeline, it really doesn't pay for these companies to fund and maintain the pipeline. This pipeline is a pipeline to energy independence for the country.[37]

The Congressional Research Service is a branch of the Library of Congress. It issued a report in November 2010[38] that stated that the United States has more fossil fuel resources than any other country in the world. In other words, if we were to start developing our own, we could create jobs and potentially we could even become a net exporter. According to the study, there are an estimated 135 billion barrels of oil that is so far undiscovered but recoverable. In addition, our natural resources include an estimated 2,047 trillion cubic feet of natural gas reserves.

But the government is stopping everyone from letting that happen. It owns huge parts of land it doesn't want to develop for exploration or drilling. Further, it's tragic if you're a businessperson. You can't spend money investing in drilling and then have the government, on a whim, pull the permit or instill a policy that will kill your business plan.

There is no doubt how important low energy prices are to industry. That's what is so maddening about Obama's anti–fossil fuel agenda and the CEOs who joined the cap-and-trade bandwagon. The following interview raises serious issues—Why would a CEO who complained about the impact of high energy prices on his company turn around and then lobby for legislation that would bring about skyrocketing energy costs??

The CEO of Dow Chemical, Andrew Liveris, was quoted on NPR in 2008 about why he had to move his operations overseas. The main reason: affordable energy. He was asked if it was the labor that was cheaper.

No, no labor, energy. Interesting enough, countries that do have an energy policy, countries like the Middle East, countries like China, countries like Russia, it's always fascinating when I give that list, you know, these are not necessarily democracies. But these are countries that are worked out that their natural resources need to be value added in their country to create meaningful high-paying jobs. That used to be the United States, but unfortunately, we've decided to restrict supply our own natural resources of this country, and of course, to increase demand with inefficiency. So, we're inefficient, we weren't in a supply ourselves, so we're at the whim of a global market price.

He was clear it's because they use their natural resources and the United States doesn't. Dow is building plants in Saudi Arabia and so is Alcoa.

The government's energy policy is very discouraging for companies, because it creates an uncertain environment, making companies ask, "Why make that bet when we can't predict what the clowns in Washington will do with energy policy?"

Why would you build in the USA when you know the Obama agenda is to make energy prices more expensive? So Dow CEO Liveris just gave up on the United States, and since he is not a citizen it does not matter to him where his company builds plants.

GREEN GONE WRONG

There is little doubt of what happens to a company when it adopts progressive business strategies. Look what happened to British Petroleum. That company caved to pressure from the left to go green years ago. The mess in the Gulf with the BP spill reminds me of another problem with our energy policies. BP is a great example of a corporation being pushed by the left to progressive policies, then being ravaged after those policies explode.

BP tried to separate itself from the other oil companies when its former head John Browne joined the global warming bandwagon and adopted the beyond-petroleum PR campaign—remember those "What's your carbon footprint?" ads? BP went left to avoid the pressure that other oil companies were getting.

Of course, when BP was in crisis, the left blamed capitalism, but of course, it should really have looked at the impact progressive policy has had on the way corporations are run. Instead of explaining the value of cheap fossil fuels to the economy BP was duped into apologizing for selling a product that was its core business.

What would have been a better use of BP's time and money: environmental and safety compliance on its rigs or a fluffy ad campaign that caved to the pressures of global warming politics? I think, based on history in the Gulf, the answer is clear.[39] At first BP was the darling of the media for advertising against its product. Soon after, however, the company had a series of environmental and safety disasters. Prior to the Deepwater Horizon explosion, the company was responsible for an explosion at a refining facility in Texas City, Texas, and BP also had oil pipeline leaks in Alaska. Those earlier instances should have been a red flag to regulators that the company was an outlier in the industry. Post explosion, the company became the poster child for corporate demonization, when really some mainstream outlet should have raised the point about wasted public relations money used to appease the left.

Guess who paid for BP's early appeasement? The other oil giants. At one point ExxonMobil was the most aggressive oil company to defend itself against the attacks from the left and what did they get in return? The company became a lightning rod for progressive activism and it buckled under the strain. Once BP jumped to the left, the rest of the companies were eventually neutered.

If I were running Exxon I'd promote the findings of a recent Congressional Research Service study that found our county is blessed with fossil fuel natural resources. The twenty-eight-page report states:

> Using only proved reserve numbers for the United States and other nations shows that the United States remains among the top nations in proved reserves of all fossil fuels taken together.[40]

If we got off this renewable energy bandwagon and made use of *recovering and using* our own natural resources, we would stimulate the economy, pay down the debt, move us toward energy security, and achieve lower energy prices. We would keep manufacturing jobs here in the United States as well. It seems so obvious. Until then, we are trapped in the green place scenario.

THE FIRST GREEN PRESIDENT

President Obama said, "If you're complaining about the price of gas and you're only getting eight miles per gallon . . . you might want to think about a trade-in."

The irony in all this is that Obama's own ride isn't so green. Remember when all the auto execs flew to Washington on separate private jets to beg for a bailout, and then drove the second time because of the political heat? Well, the president isn't zipping around in a Prius, though he claims he asked for a green car. The U.S. Secret Service said his limo is exempt from the directive that federal cars be subjected to the green standards laid out when Obama took office.

Still, he's ramming electricity from renewable energy down our throats and now it seems he's willing to drive up gas prices to force us into buying electric cars. He wants the government and U.S. companies to switch to electric cars too—again at the taxpayers' expense, of course. He's initiated the Clean Fleets Partnership, which will give companies assistance as a swap for lowering oil usage.

There is no question that energy policy will be a major driver in the next election. The GOP already knocked a bit of wind out of the president's plan by gaining power in the 2010 midterms. Alternative energy is appealing because the American public doesn't fully understand how intentionally the wool is being pulled over their eyes with regard to coal. But soaring utility and gas prices will shine a spotlight on energy, overseas drilling, and our need to be energy self-sufficient. Unpopularity and energy prices are a team in an election fight.

Either way, President Obama should end his war on fossil fuels. He should change course and demand that the EPA immediately stop his plan to regulate greenhouse gas emissions, ease other EPA regulations targeting coal-fired utilities, and ease drilling restrictions in the Gulf of Mexico. He needs to encourage industry to invest domestically and the only way to do that is to remove the uncertainty that exists around the exploration of our natural resources. Business, except for his pals in wind and alternative energy, can't trust the policies, can't create jobs, and can't waste time and money. By now, Obama should realize his pledge to make energy prices "skyrocket" is really bad for the country. He should know his policies are simply supporting the rich who have a stake in the alternative game. But then again, given Obama's anticolonial views he knows how bad his anti–fossil fuel agenda is and that's his end game.

Perhaps Congress should step in and rein in his powers. One step in that direction is the Energy Tax Prevention Act of 2011, meant to control the EPA's heavy-handed attempt to use the Clean Air Act to stop carbon emissions. It's drawn some bipartisan support in the Senate but needs more support to become law.

And if his power can't be stopped from within, then energy companies should go on the offensive. Oil and utility companies are going to get blamed for high energy prices because of a shortage of supply. A true capitalist response would be for the companies to tell the public why there is a

shortage: because of a combination of government regulation and an anti-drilling, -mining, and -exploration policy.
Oil executives need to inform the public instead of letting
the government and the left do the brainwashing. They
are going to get blamed when prices go higher, so the best
decision is to fight for what is right.

CRONY CAPITALISM

Your green is for their green: The bottom line is that you're
getting the short end of the stick on green energy and
special interests are winning. Your hard-earned dollars are
funding their portfolios and lavish lifestyles. You are being
scared into thinking that green is good and told coal and
drilling are bad. Don't buy it. It's at best coercive, at worst
corrupt. Pure and simple, this energy push was and is
crony capitalism. Sadly, if it were not for the greedy CEOs
and politicians involved, turning their backs on the USA
to profit from traditional energy sources, we might have
a sound energy policy. As long as coal and oil prices soar,
who cares what country corporations build their plants in
and do business from? Not Immelt, or Doerr or Obama
for that matter. Nope. They all worked both ends.

The tide is slowly turning against the green bubble.
Even legendary investor Jim Chanos is shorting renewable
energy. Immelt's feeling the squeeze from his board and
shareholders and the negative PR is beginning to make
him change gears. Did they think this would work? Did
they think they could pull the wool over the eyes of the

likes of the Tea Party and activists watching? They're all so arrogant and greedy that when cap-and-trade was in play, these guys had the gall to request not just the money that came with selling emission output, but also back credit for unused emissions!

This green thing is tarnished. Americans might have briefly fallen for this stuff, but the curtain has been pulled back on the real motivation. Even Kyoto is crumbling. It's time to stop this nonsense and go long on America. It's time to focus on keeping people in the coal and oil industries employed. Did you know that if we focus on what we have available to us in terms of energy needs, we could be energy independent, and not suffer through the pricing we have now at the pumps and enjoy cheaper utility prices? If we rely only on our resources and up our offshore drilling and oil and natural gas drilling and maximize our coal and shale options, we'd be in great shape. We have more fossil fuel natural resources than any other country. It's time to wake up to the whitewashing that elites and Obama have done on us under the guise of saving the planet. Save our jobs. Save our economy. Save companies from going overseas for cheap energy.

Save America.

SEVEN

The Dangers of an Unhealthy Liberal Agenda

I love these members, they get up and say, "Read the bill" . . . What good is reading the bill if it's a thousand pages and you don't have two days and two lawyers to find out what it means after you read the bill?

—*Congressman John Conyers (D-MI), in response to Republican critics of the health care bill, who charged that its supporters had not even read it*

There has been a notable shift in our discussion about health care. We don't talk about ways of using innovation and advanced technology to cut costs and improve the actual health of Americans. We don't talk about free market approaches that would increase competition and cut costs. We don't talk about malpractice reform that would reduce the volume of unnecessary tests that contribute to the unsustainable price tag of health care. Instead, we talk about the president's plan—his backward vision that effectively keeps us under the government thumb, enslaving us to a cold and uncaring bureaucracy, while exploding the public debt.

ObamaCare isn't about medicine for your children. It is not about improving the benefits you get at work. And it does not help prevent illness in order to limit health problems down the road. Rather, ObamaCare is about Obama's overriding philosophy that decisions are better left to the government than with the individual and that the state is a better arbiter of how to allocate our health care dollars than the free market. Obama's vision is one of a traditional liberal: to expand the entitlement state to cover health care coverage through an existing infrastructure. Once in control, however, Americans will be empowering bureaucrats to deny treatment and services, especially to the most vulnerable, in an effort to control costs.

The United States is an exceptional country—we are "a shining city upon a hill." [1] Americans are extremely compassionate and generous. When disaster strikes anywhere in the world, we are the first to jump into action, providing aid and our expertise. It doesn't matter if it is on another continent or as close to home as New Orleans. We are there—committed to helping people help themselves. We can do this because it's part of our national character and because our free market economy has provided us with a degree of wealth that gives many of us disposable income that can be allocated to charity. Our economic strength has made us the single most powerful nation on earth.

But we are at a crossroads. Do we want to continue in this direction, or do we want to become a nation of people enslaved to our national debt, weakened by our country's gross spending habits?

ObamaCare is also about spending money we don't have and it will greatly contribute to our national debt. Sure, it has a nice ring to it—the government will be your health care backstop, ensuring that you and your kids will be safe and secure. The government will not be doing this. The government is going to be pouring money into unworkable, inefficient bureaucracies and in doing so, it will stake claim to the biggest entitlement expansion since the 1960s.

Make no mistake about it: The promises of ObamaCare are terribly misleading. Name just one government program that has delivered a cost-efficient and reliable service? The United States Postal Service? Amtrak? Compassion, caring, and fiscal efficiency are not characteristics of government enterprises—period. The *care* in ObamaCare is about Obama *caring* about a progressive legacy that will greatly expand government control over lives. Oh, yes, your care will suffer. If tragedy strikes and your child needs special medical treatment, how long will it take to get an appointment with a specialist—assuming there will be one to find?

By the time many of the adverse consequences of ObamaCare kick in, Obama won't be in office, but on the speaking circuit cashing in while the rest of us suffer. Obama is an elite, and after his presidency he will never have to worry about money or not being able to buy the best health care for his family. Meanwhile, you will be struggling to figure out how to get quality medical services.

The liberal agenda is a double-edged sword. Sure, it always sounds nice. Clean and renewable energy from the wind and sun. Accessible, affordable, and quality health care for all regardless of your employment or health status. It has a feel-good kind of ring to it. The government will always be there to take care of you. If times get tough: The government will pay for your health care. The government will protect your mortgage. The government will give you jobs, money, food, and housing. But the fact remains, the government can't pay for this agenda. The liberal agenda is thick with sweeping generalizations and false promises of hope. The only consistency is its failure to deliver yet with such a dismal record. Too many Americans get lured into the progressive fantasy that through the grace of big government man can create heaven on earth.

Someone has to pay these ObamaCare bills. Sure, Obama will pay his personal share—but he can afford it with his million-dollar-plus income. It is me, you, and our children and grandchildren who will pay. What we are paying today is only a down payment for the future cost of the program over the long term. Its cost will drain our economy, raise our taxes, and lower our standard of living and for all of that we will beg a bureaucracy for treatment. That's what I mean when I say Obama is ensuring we will always be slaves on the government plantation. We need to break these chains. We need to send those overseers packing. We need to become masters in our own homes and control our own destinies. We need to be responsible for buying our own health insurance and take responsibility for our lifestyle choices. And most of all, we need to recognize that the *care* in ObamaCare is an illusion, just like the rest of the progressive agenda.

HEALTH CARE REFORM

In March 2010, President Obama signed two pieces of legislation passed by Congress to address health care in the United States. Combined, the Patient Protection and Affordable Care Act[2] and the Health Care and Education Reconciliation Act of 2010[3] were intended to fundamentally change the nature, scope, and implementation of medical care in the United States. As one commentator explained, the measure was broadly sweeping in nature, addressing many facets of health care. It would "require most Americans to have health insurance coverage; would add 16 million people to the Medicaid rolls; and would subsidize private coverage for low- and middle-income people." Moreover, private insurers would be regulated "more closely, banning practices such as denial of care for pre-existing conditions."[4] At the heart of the legislation was an attempt by government to try to improve health care by reforming insurance coverage. Extensive regulations were adopted to mandate who can offer different types of insurance and how.

As the Heritage Foundation's Brian Blase explained in his analysis of the effect of the legislation one year after its adoption, its costs certainly outweigh its benefits:

Deneen Borelli

Obamacare has increased government control of Americans' health care choices, raised the cost of insurance, forced insurers to stop offering child-only policies, broken the promise that an individual can keep his insurance unaltered, and bailed out underfunded union early-retiree health care plans.[5]

In theory, the changes adopted by Congress were based on a desire to ensure that quality health care would be available to all Americans at an affordable cost. As we know, however, if it sounds too good to be true it probably is. ObamaCare really drove that saying home.

Recognizing that big business was the key to the legislative success, Obama appealed to the short-term self-interest of insurance and drug companies to convert potential adversaries to allies. Big business played a key role in ramming ObamaCare down our throats.

What was striking about the health care package was the process—the legislative levers and tricks that were played by the Democrat majority and how it was rushed through Congress. During Obama's election campaign that screamed out for *hope* and *change*, he made a commitment to the American people that he would work with people from all political parties. He promised an unprecedented transparency to his legislative initiatives. There was an emphasis on a bipartisan approach to politics. We expected that this meant he would consider the point of view of both Republicans and Democrats and would work together. Clearly we were duped. When the House

186

of Representatives voted on the health care reform package, not one Republican supported the measure. The vote was 219–212. Some Democrats went against their party by voting against it, but not even one Republican accepted it as a credible solution to the health care crisis facing this country.[6]

Is this what Obama meant by reaching across the aisle? Why shut out Republicans from his plan? Obama could have delayed the passage of the health care measure in order to ensure that Republicans had an opportunity to participate in its drafting to modify its terms and conditions. Why didn't he want a better legislative measure with cross-party support to ensure its legitimacy and future? Not with Obama. Empowered by an overwhelming majority in Congress—it's his way or the highway.

Obama was stubborn about modifying his plan. The February 25, 2010, "Health Care Summit" was a meeting between the top leaders from both parties, brought together to hash out the differences in the proposed plans and the president's one. When Republican Senator John McCain voiced his concerns about the way health care had been handled—with backroom plans and little transparency, Obama fired back harshly: "Let me just make this point, John, because we are not campaigning anymore," and he added, "The election's over."[7]

There was a point during the daylong event when the president became sort of testy, revealing his true end game, and making clear that the meeting was a charade, that he wasn't there to negotiate. He said, "We've got to go ahead and move forward on a vote."[8]

The reason that the president wanted this measure adopted quickly, regardless of the opposition's concerns, was to hide its many defects before the congressional clock struck twelve. The longer the debates extended in Congress, the more likely the American people would have the opportunity to see the bill's vast weaknesses. And there are plenty of them. I have a few major concerns about this health care reform, all of which will keep us on the government plantation rather than give us a chance to choose our own health care needs and priorities.

EXCESSIVE COSTS

Estimates vary as to the actual cost of the program. In part, there is discrepancy in the numbers because the estimates are based on different time periods. But however you look at them, the dollars are staggering. It's estimated that the cost of the entire health care package in its first ten years of operation is about $2 trillion when it comes fully into effect from 2014 to 2023.[9] Our insurance premiums are anticipated to rise by almost a third, from 10 percent to 13 percent, and the gross domestic product spent on health care costs would jump from 17 percent to 21 percent by 2019.[10]

And the huge costs are not being disproportionately affected by just the wealthy who might be able to afford the added expenses to their otherwise high household costs. We are all paying and paying. As one study shows, those who can least afford the expense for so-called "improved" health care bear the largest burden:

> A Kaiser Family Foundation survey of employers last year found that average premiums for an employer-provided family policy, which is more likely to be the type of comprehensive coverage required by Obama-Care, was $13,375, about 25 percent of the median household income of $52,000.
>
> That $13,375 family policy costs the same for both lower- and higher-income workers. So if the mandate is a tax, it's equivalent to a 50 percent income tax on a family making $25,000 a year but a 10 percent income tax on a family making $130,000 a year. Talk about regressive taxes! [11]

In other words, the enormous expenses that we are being subjected to in the name of improved health care are bankrupting the family.

Nor are the costs simply limited to the amount of money we are going to be paying for health care under ObamaCare. This health care initiative forced on us by the Obama administration has significant costs for our economy as well. The health care legislation that was supposed to improve the quality and access to health care is going to push many families into the unemployment line. That's right—because of this measure, tens of thousands of Americans already struggling are going to find themselves without a job. And if you think this is just some kind of conservative nonsense, look at the source of this statistic. In February 2011, Doug Elmendorf, the director of the Congressional Budget Office, acknowledged that by 2020–21, employment would be reduced by 800,000 positions because of the health care law.[12]

Is this really how we should tackle health care problems? Aren't the costs too high? Paying higher taxes and letting the government ring up the deficit for lousy medical care is suicidal. Higher unemployment with fewer Americans generating tax revenue will only accelerate our deficit and debt problems. Clearly this is not the direction in which we should be heading. Instead individuals should be empowered to decide how they spend their money.

Along with this command and control from our government comes a hefty price tag for states. Although the federal government is expected to pay for ObamaCare within the first three years of the program, states will be on the hook to pay millions of dollars for many years to come.[13]

An estimated 16 million Americans are expected to be added to Medicaid, a system that's already burdened and has its share of problems. And that number might be on the low side: A flaw in the legislation expands Medicaid coverage to include even more Americans, perhaps as many as 24.7 million, which will increase the cost by billions.[14]

Common sense dictates that considering the waste, fraud, and abuse of the current Medicaid system, ObamaCare will only add to these woes. How can states possibly budget and plan for such an exorbitant expense, given the fact that most states are cash strapped in part due to current entitlement expenses?

ACCESS

The notion that the Obama initiative on health care reform was some kind of cure-all to solve the health crisis facing this country was absurd. Although one of the president's main objectives in this program was to ensure that everyone would have access to medical insurance, he completely failed. In fact, by 2019, it is estimated that approximately 23 million Americans will still not have access to health insurance.[15] This despite all of the money that Obama is throwing at his plan.

And what is most disconcerting about this mess is that the very people the program is supposed to target—those most vulnerable—are the ones left without much hope. Take for example the fiasco known as the high-risk pools. This initiative was a short-term program designed to ensure that those with preexisting conditions who were not able to buy health care insurance would have some type of coverage. But the entire measure was poorly thought out and designed to fail from the start. It was created to act as a temporary measure until private insurance companies initiated similar programs in 2014.

Five billion dollars was set aside to provide funding for states for this high-risk pools program. But the funding was a drop in the bucket compared to what was needed.

It would cover only 200,000 to 400,000 people or only about 10 percent of those who had preexisting illnesses.[16] The Congressional Budget Office preliminary estimates indicate that the initiative is underfunded in the sense that the actual cost of the program will be 10 to 15 billion dollars even though the cap is set at 5 billion.[17] And this figure includes only those who apply to participate in it. As the CBO explains, many will not enroll in the program "as many potential applicants will be discouraged from enrolling by the premium they would have to pay and the cost-sharing requirements they would face in the program. Others might be eligible for the program but not aware of it."[18]

And what are the consequences? As Representative John Boehner, Speaker of the House of Representatives and leading critic of the Obama health care initiative, explains, there are considerable downsides that far outweigh any benefits. Such an approach "will lead to higher premiums and more limited access for patients, and higher costs for taxpayers."[19] The people who really need medical care will not be served. Access will not be enhanced. Everyone will pay more and effectively have less ability to get quality care. And the problem will still exist. It's not that people like Speaker Boehner and I don't want to have this issue addressed. People with preexisting medical conditions who can't access the health care they need present a serious problem. But the Obama plan is not the way to resolve the problem, because we will all pay more for fewer services without actually addressing the real issues.

Sounds like another big-government failure to me.

Nor are people with preexisting illnesses the only ones who will face such limited access to health care and insurance. Children will also not be better off. In the past, families could purchase health care insurance for a particular child. This child-only health insurance policy let moms and dads choose how to best use their family income and target their priorities. It was a great private insurance solution to a thorny issue.

But the Obama plan changed all of this. It layered red tape on more red tape to mandate that insurance companies sell these single coverage plans for individual children to everyone who applied regardless of whether the applicants had a preexisting medical problem. So what do you think happened? Do you think that people rushed out and gained access to this health care for their children? Do you think more children were given coverage and that access was improved?

What happened here is typical of these poorly thought-out initiatives when government provides only Band-Aid solutions to serious crises. As one analysis indicates, the consequences of the Obama "solution" have effectively created a crisis by limiting access and choice for parents who want policies to cover a child:

One year later, an unintended consequence of the ban on considering preexisting conditions is that insurers in at least 34 states have exited the market and 20 states now have no insurers offering child-only plans. The insurers fear that the ban encourages parents to wait until their children are sick before looking for insurance coverage.

Insurers have dropped out of the market even though the U.S. Department of Health and Human Services (HHS) has ruled that insurers can limit enrollment to open-enrollment periods as long as insurers do not "selectively deny enrollment for children with a preexisting condition while accepting enrollment from other children outside of the open-enrollment period." Moreover, in response to insurers pulling out of the child-only health insurance market, the Administration has decided that insurers "can adjust their rates based on health status until 2014, to the extent state law allows."[20]

Exactly how are these results of the Obama plan considered an improvement for children?

In other words, the Obama health care initiative did exactly the opposite of what it intended to address. It wanted to ensure access for those most vulnerable, such as those with preexisting illnesses or children. Instead it created bigger problems than existed previously. Ironically, many of the extreme left were unhappy since Obama failed to deliver the progressive health care Holy Grail—universal coverage, also known as single payer. While Obama made great strides to advance the progressive agenda he fell short of the goal line. Making public policy that reduces individual liberty is not good for the country. In fact, it entrenches and expands the very enslavement we need to end.

Rather than solve these issues, the Obama administration made them worse by expanding the role of an intrusive government in the way of what should ideally be a private transaction between individuals and their doctors. Increasing the reliance of Americans on government services as crucial as health care is another way of putting people on the government plantation. They become slaves to the system. We need Americans to be freethinking individuals making choices in their own best interest. We want people to be able to help themselves and their families. Independence—not dependence—and economic empowerment are what is needed to improve access to health care.

THE REAL BENEFICIARIES

There are two categories of people who benefit from ObamaCare. First, the Democratic politicians make big gains. Obama and his elected pals in the Congress get bragging rights for having "fixed" the system by giving people the illusion of something for nothing. Giving away freebies as a means to get votes has been the key to progressive politicians for years. By making false promises they are able to shore up their electoral support before they go to the polls in 2012. That their so-called solutions are short term that actually set us back further doesn't really matter to them. Kicking the economic can down the road is a favored politician's trick. Most likely they will be out of office by the time the economic consequences kick in. It is the news cycle and how they can portray themselves to the voters that matter most.

Don't get me wrong; more "doctors" are being hired under the Obama administration. But they are the high-paid spin doctors tucked away in the bowels of big consulting and lobby firms. Their job is to manipulate the regulatory system to get a competitive advantage for their clients. These lobbying antics will only serve the special interests, leaving the rest of us out to dry.

Next, big businesses wins. The insurance and the pharmaceutical companies are also big winners from Obama-Care. Despite Obama's rhetoric about special-interest influence in public policy and the need for transparency, the president was the master of backroom deals.

Big business loved the initiatives that Obama introduced because his programs were going to line their already deep pockets. When the Clintons were in the White House and they tried to introduce health care reform, the insurance and drug companies effectively blocked them. They mounted an aggressive lobbying campaign against HillaryCare and killed it.

But that opposition was nowhere to be found with ObamaCare. The insurance and drug companies loved the potential of Obama*Care* because the law would boost their profits. They were and still are in the Obama administration's back pocket.

Powerful interest groups seeking profits are willing to follow their narrow short-term interests despite the moral consequences of their actions. If I can recognize the serious fiscal consequences and lower quality of care from Obama-Care so can the heads of the insurance and pharmaceutical companies. With a government already so much involved in their day-to-day operations it was easier to go with the flow and not challenge the status quo. As the old expression goes, "Don't bite the hand that feeds you."

It came as no surprise to me that after lobbying on ObamaCare, the health insurers are defending the law. The CEO of Cigna, who according to Reuters is one of the largest U.S. health insurance providers, is opposed to fundamentally restructuring the ObamaCare initiative at this time. David Cordani explained at the Reuters Health Care Summit in November 2010, "I don't think it is in our society's best interest to expend energy in repealing the law." He noted, "Our country expended over a year of sweat equity around the formation of it."[21]

Another saying goes, "Better the devil you know than you don't." Oddly to many, big business is not truly capitalistic. Competing in the free market is hard, so many companies prefer using their access to government to guarantee sales while locking out the competition.

The chief strategy officer of GlaxoSmithKline, David Redfern, has argued that the new health care law created "a stable, predictable environment, however painful it has been in the short term."[22]

The insurance companies like the ObamaCare program for a number of reasons. First, it will increase the amount of premiums they receive from the American people. Approximately 30 million Americans are going to become new health insurance policyholders under the ObamaCare initiative by 2014. Otherwise they face a fine.[23] As one analyst explains, this will help enhance the bottom line of health insurance providers, who expect that the rise in the premiums will exceed the payouts they are going to need to make:

> Under Obamacare, for at least a few years the insurers hope to get One Last Windfall—namely, profits from the influx of previously-uninsured Americans whose premiums will be paid, or at least subsidized, by taxpayers. Here, the insurers are relying on the likelihood that the inflow of new premiums will, for a year or two at least, greatly outweigh the outflow of money they will have to spend caring for these new subscribers. Obviously, they will use every trick in their well-worn book to stave off expenditures for these new subscribers for as long as they can, but if they actually knew how to avoid paying health care costs indefinitely, they wouldn't be seeking a government bailout today. In any case, an inflow of new subscribers will be a very temporary source of profit for insurers. Hence, at best it is One Last Windfall.[24]

In other words, this means that at least for a short time, there is going to be an influx of payments from taxpayers to insurance companies. At least on a short-term basis, the cash going into the insurance companies will exceed its costs. They aren't going to question Obama's plan now while there is money to be made from the initiative.

Insurance companies, however, also like the Obama-Care program because it gives incentives to overinsure healthy people while ignoring those who have serious medical conditions.[25] As John Goodman and Bob Moffit explain, this approach is nothing short of backward thinking. They argue that instead "of requiring insurers to 'ignore' the fact that some people are sicker and more costly to insure, we should adopt a system that compensates them for the higher expected costs. Ideally, this system would make a high-cost enrollee just as attractive to an insurer as low-cost one."[26]

The pharmaceutical industry desperately wanted ObamaCare. Their backroom deal with Obama involved the industry being protected from drug re-importation—that is, selling drugs sold in other countries that are cheaper than the price charged in the United States—and the industry was shielded from negotiating the prices of drugs being sold to the government through Medicare. The industry also committed to pay $80 billion over ten years[27] to financially support the health care reform effort. With that deal in hand the drug industry trade association allocated $150 million for TV commercials to sell the public on Obama's health care plan.[28]

Of course, Obama's heath care plan overhaul rush to the finish line had numerous problems contained in the over two-thousand-page bill. Not only did Representative John Conyers (D-MI) not want to read the bill, then House Speaker Nancy Pelosi (D-CA) declined to reveal the details of the bill when she said, "But we have to pass the bill so that you can find out what is in it, away from the fog of controversy."[29] Perhaps Pelosi did not know the details or she did know and she was hiding the bill's elements from the American people. Either way this is an extremely poor example of Pelosi representing Americans.

The law passed, and now we are finding out those details and they are not looking good! The reality of "what is in it" is now in full sight with respect to the waivers being given to unions and corporations.

These waivers are being given because the one-size-fits-all central planning of health care envisioned by Obama-Care does not fit numerous individual situations. One of the major selling points of ObamaCare was the notion that individuals would not lose the health care coverage that they had. Oops! After the bill passed, hundreds of waivers affecting millions of workers are being issued to prevent the embarrassment of a major promise being broken. In fact, it is estimated that almost a "million workers won't get a consumer protection in the U.S. health reform law meant to cap insurance costs because the government exempted their employers."[30]

According to *USA Today*, thirty companies and unions were given these waivers. The Department of Health and Human Services (HHS) explained that these waivers were issued to these organizations "so workers with such plans wouldn't lose coverage from employers who might choose instead to drop health insurance altogether."

In other words, these workers had health insurance

through their employers, but because of the ObamaCare plan, they were going to lose their coverage. Employers could no longer afford to maintain the costs for their workers under the new rules imposed by the Obama administration. And in the process, if the waivers weren't issued, they would have effectively shifted this responsibility to the taxpayer.

Not surprisingly, the biggest waiver was awarded to the United Federation of Teachers in New York for over 350,000 teachers for a one-year period.[31]

The United Agricultural Benefit Trust, a cooperative in California, was given a waiver for 17,347 people, while companies like McDonald's received a waiver for 115,000.[32] Is this really the kind of health care reform we want? If the private sector was providing coverage for its workers, why do we want the Obama administration effectively dismantling it?

Some states were also issued waivers. A *New York Times* article from February 2011 indicates that Florida, New Jersey, Tennessee, and Ohio were given waivers to allow health insurance companies "to continue offering less generous benefits than they would otherwise be required to provide this year under the new federal health care law":

Under the law and rules issued by the administration, health plans this year must generally provide at least $750,000 in coverage for essential benefits like hospital care, doctors' services and prescription drugs. In states granted the waivers, many health plans with much lower annual limits on coverage may continue to operate.[33]

These four states had provisions "that required or encouraged health plans to offer limited-benefit coverage."[34]

And it seems some of Pelosi's constituents didn't like ObamaCare once they discovered what was in it. "Of the 204 new Obamacare waivers President Barack Obama's administration approved in April, 38 are for fancy eateries, hip nightclubs and decadent hotels in House Minority Leader Nancy Pelosi's Northern California district." In all, entities in Pelosi's district got 20 percent of the waivers issued that month.[35]

Apparently, the Obama administration got tired of the waiver mania and announced that the Health and Human Services department would stop accepting new applications for health care waivers on September 22, 2011. According to the Government Accountability Office report, as of June 14, 2011, HHS had approved the vast majority (95 percent) of the 1,415 waivers it reviewed regarding annual limits on health benefits. The new and renewed waivers will be valid until the start of 2014, when the primary elements of ObamaCare will be effective.[36, 37]

As time goes by it is increasingly apparent that Obama-Care is a failure. Not only are states, unions, and companies seeking waivers but also many employers are planning to dump employee health care coverage once the elements of ObamaCare become effective in 2014.

According to a survey of 1,300 employers published

in *McKinsey Quarterly*, "At least 30% of employers would gain economically from dropping coverage, even if they completely compensated employees for the change through other benefit offerings or higher salaries." [38]

Even some Democrats recognize the problems with ObamaCare and the potential for employers to dump health care coverage for employees because ObamaCare exists. Appearing on MSNBC's *Morning Joe*, Howard Dean, former Democratic National Committee chairman, agreed with the findings of the McKinsey & Co. survey. Dean said, "The fact is it is very good for small business. There was a McKinsey study, which the Democrats don't like, but I do, and I think it's true. Most small businesses are not going to be in the health insurance business anymore after this thing goes into effect." [39]

Again, we have to ask, who are the actual beneficiaries of the ObamaCare program? What was its purpose? Aside from these political questions, the number and diversity of groups seeking waivers and the eagerness of employers to drop health care coverage are proof it's a bad law.

THE HEALTH CARE PLANTATION

The president should respect the will of the people. He needs to demonstrate that he can be an effective leader.

According to the Rasmussen Reports national survey that has been tracking attitudes toward the ObamaCare program, "51% of Likely U.S. Voters now at least somewhat favor repeal of the law." In other words, half of the voting population wants this measure removed. And they want it repealed for good reasons such as "Most voters still believe free market competition rather than more government regulation is the better way to reduce the cost of health care in America." [40]

Some in Washington's circles get that democracy means reflecting the will of the people. John Boehner certainly understands. He has tirelessly sought to point out the inconsistencies and absurdities underpinning the Obama-Care policy. He is working for the people, not just for his reelection. I couldn't agree more when he says that officials elected to Congress should reflect the will of the people and repeal this ridiculous health-spending program. By adopting this health care measure, he noted, "We will have shattered those bonds of trust [of the American people]." [41]

Importantly, the unpopularity of ObamaCare has contributed to a rise in state opposition to the law. More than half of the states are suing the government over the constitutionality of ObamaCare.

In 2012 the U.S. Supreme Court will rule on the challenges that worked through the lower courts that the individual mandate of ObamaCare is an overreach of federal power and therefore is unconstitutional. [42]

The ObamaCare initiative is more aptly named Obama-Spend and Control. Its costs are excessive and ensure that generations to come will be enslaved to paying off the national debt. Empowering a government bureaucracy to control our health care choices is extremely dangerous, especially for those of us concerned about liberty. We the people will get higher costs for reduced health care services.

Only I can take care of my family and myself. The government is not responsible for my health. And frankly, I don't want it to be. Bureaucrats make bad choices and think about the short term rather than my long-term well-being. ObamaSpend and Control should be scrapped before it causes further harm to our existing system. The government plantation is no place for us to reside. We need to unshackle the chains that bind us to the elites in Washington who think about themselves rather than the people of this great nation.

EIGHT

Playing the Race Card

That's what it's all sort of couched in—this secret
agenda. And when they say, or Gingrich says, [Obama
is] a Lao Tribesman, it's all sort of code.

—Mad Men *star, actor Jon Hamm*

I t's actually quite clever for the left to make the discussion
about the Tea Party about race. It distracts everyone from
having to talk about the real toxic issues that Obama's
administration is bringing to the table. It revs up emotions, stifles legitimate debate about limited government
and wasted spending, and it makes people uncomfortable.

I mean, always pointing out race, applying labels, discussing race in every conversation dealing with the Tea
Party—isn't that a little racist in and of itself? Claiming
every anti-Obama sentiment or disagreement with his actions is racist? Isn't that problematic? The left can't have a

conversation about policy with the Tea Party because they can't argue away their mess. It's simply not possible. So instead they have to throw stones as a distraction.

So according to one actor the Tea Party is speaking in code. Code? The Tea Party is speaking in racist code? No, but the left is desperate to keep the Tea Party from success, so they started a smear campaign and they used race to do it. They called the Tea Party movement "racist." But that is just a big attempt to keep the movement down. This movement is rapidly gaining momentum and the left is scared. People involved are becoming educated, getting motivated, and forcing politicians to actually listen. Citizens are reading up on history and studying the Constitution to really understand how policies are made. The movement is changing the country. It's making people realize they have a voice, they can be involved in the policy process, and they—as individuals and as part of a larger movement—can have an impact. The Tea Party has awoken the people from a slumber. People are fed up with career politicians and politics as usual. The Tea Party is challenging status quo politics in order to change the way Washington elites do their business.

The left is working hard to block this new movement's progress, using aggressive tactics in an attempt to impede the force and significance of this social and political powerhouse. There was, frankly, a lot of doubt surrounding the movement early on. FreedomWorks, an organization that "recruits, educates, trains and mobilizes millions of volunteer activists to fight for less government, lower taxes, and more freedom," became an early believer in the

Tea Party despite the concerns and is now a driving force behind the Tea Party nationwide.

It's interesting: When my husband and I first got started with the Tea Party, there was some discussion about a conservative movement having rallies. The prevailing wisdom was that rallies were a thing of the left. So it was risky to take that tack, but Matt Kibbe, FreedomWorks' president and CEO, took a chance with the 9/12 March on DC on September 12, 2009. There have been thousands of rallies nationwide. The Tea Party movement has changed the way politics operates by starting a conservative grassroots movement. Now look at us! To date, the movement is responsible for making a number of Democratic incumbents retire and making others run for their political lives.

I guess it shouldn't have been a surprise that once we gained any sort of momentum the race card would be the first card played as the Tea Party emerged. With the media obsessed with racism coupled with the first black president, race was sure to be an issue and the old progressive smear campaign would step right up.

True to form, early on in the Tea Party's development, MSNBC and its hosts and guests were actively trying to label the Tea Party movement as racist. For example, actress Janeane Garofalo claimed that the movement was about racism against a black president and she used the term "rednecks" to describe Tea Party members. The former chairman of the House Ways and Means Committee Charlie Rangel said during the health care debate that "bias" and "prejudice" against President Obama are the reasons why there's so much opposition to the health care proposal. Rangel also said, "You don't see any black folks in these groups. Ever, ever, ever, ever, ever."

In January 2010, MSNBC's Chris Matthews made the claim too that everyone at the Tea Party rallies, like the one held in September 2009 in Washington, is white. In a discussion with Mark McKinnon of the *Daily Beast* and Susan Page of *USA Today*, Matthews said: "And they're monochromatic, right? . . . Meaning they're all white. All of them—every single one of them—are white."

Ummm—I'm not. I spoke at the 9/12 March on DC in 2009 and many other rallies and conferences nationwide.

You know, I've spoken on this often and I truly think there is only one way to address these racist allegations: hit them head-on. Swing for the fences and knock the ball out of the park. Here are the frankest words I have for the closed-minded folks who call me, a black woman, and my organization—racist.

To Janeane Garofalo: "My neck is not red!"

To Charlie Rangel: "The movement is about the policies, not race, and—oh, by the way, Charlie, pay your taxes!"

To Maxine Waters and Dianne Watson: "Socialism is evil."

To John Conyers: "Read the bill!"

I find it disgraceful that Nancy Pelosi exploited blacks' past fights for civil rights with the progressive goal of making health care a right. And really: to link arms with Representative John Lewis and members of the congressional leadership to march to the Capitol in protest, somehow mimicking the 1965 march from Selma to Montgomery, Alabama, in the wake of the "Bloody Sunday" attack on civil rights marchers earlier that month . . . well, that was insulting and patronizing to those who fought for civil rights that day.

IT NEVER ENDS

Representative Steve Cohen crossed a big line with his comparison of Tea Partiers to members of the KKK, furthering his partisan goal to demonize and discredit ordinary citizens—people who attend rallies, town hall meetings, make phone calls, and visit their representatives with the simple, legitimate concern of wanting to preserve their liberty. The Tea Party movement is making a positive difference for the direction of our country in a manner that would make our Founding Fathers proud, and the derogatory comments targeting these freedom-loving citizens really only shames those hurling them. And it is especially odd that Representative Cohen was the one hurling the mud this time. In 2008, he suffered through an opponent publicly comparing him to a Klansman. Nikki Tinker, a primary opponent, ran television ads that placed a photo of Cohen next to one of a Klansman. Tinker based the implication against Cohen on the fact that, as a member of the Center City Commission, Cohen once voted against exhuming the body of the late Confederate general (and KKK founder) Nathan Bedford Forrest from Forrest Park in Memphis.

Deneen Borelli

He certainly must not have enjoyed that. Is Cohen so tone-deaf that he is willing to immediately turn around and use the same vitriol against others?

While appearing on *The Young Turks* radio show on Sirius XM satellite radio on April 1, 2010, Cohen said Tea Party rally participants "are, kind of, without robes and hoods" and "against any type of diversity." He suggested the motivation behind the Tea Parties are not necessarily issues but "to be against Barack Obama and Rahm Emanuel and the different people." Different people? That sounds racist itself, to me.

And let me take this opportunity to remind Representative Cohen that the late Democrat Senator Robert Byrd was a Klansman with "robes and hoods."

Byrd additionally called the sight of people protesting on the U.S. Capitol grounds on the day of the Sunday ObamaCare vote in the House of Representatives "a very sad scene on America." Interestingly, Cohen represents a majority-black congressional district in Memphis.

In the wake of the historic elections in 2010 that were propelled by the Tea Party movement, it seemed the false claims of racism had run their course. But in the summer of 2011, as Obama's poll numbers were falling and the failure of his economic policies became more obvious, the racism rhetoric reared its ugly head again.

During a Congressional Black Caucus Job Tour, Representative André Carson (D-IN) made the outrageous claim that the Tea Party wanted to stop blacks from achieving social progress. "This is the effort that we are seeing of Jim Crow. Some of these folks in Congress right now would love to see us as second-class citizens. Some of them in Congress right now with this Tea Party movement would love to see you and me . . . hanging on a tree," said Carson. "Some of them right now in Congress right now are comfortable with where we were fifty or sixty years ago."[1]

Tragically, Carson was not the lone agent in the attack on the Tea Party movement. During the same Congressional Black Caucus Job Tour, Representative Maxine Waters (D-CA) said, "This is a tough game. You can't be intimidated. You can't be frightened. And as far as I'm concerned, the 'tea party' can go straight to Hell."[2] As if the attack from the black political establishment was not enough, Hollywood got into the race card act. In response to a question from CNN's Piers Morgan, Academy Award–winning actor Morgan Freeman said, "The tea parties who are controlling the Republican party . . . their stated policy, publicly stated, is to do whatever it takes to see to it that Obama only serves one term. What underlines that? Screw the country. We're going to do whatever we can to get this black man out of here."[3]

Freeman's comment had special meaning to me and I will admit that Freeman is a great actor. Years ago, I had the opportunity to see him live in action. I was excited and proud of my role as an extra in the 1989 biographical movie *Lean on Me*, starring Freeman. He played the role of high school principal Joe Clark. The movie was about an inner-city high school plagued by numerous problems—particularly gang violence, drugs, and poor test scores. I had connected with him from that experience. Because of my personal experience on the set and from watching

Deneen Borelli

this film so many times over the years, I actually looked up to Freeman.

That is, until now.

Based on this recent history of race card politics I fear the upcoming election will set a low mark for unsubstantiated claims targeting the Tea Party movement from the black elite, and I pray these comments don't further ignite racial tension.

DISPEL THE MYTH

It's simply time to dispel this ridiculous myth that the Tea Party movement is about race. I am living, breathing proof that it's not. It's about issues, it's about limited government, and it's about the progressive elites seeking to control our lives by expanding the bureaucracy. Not race.

Every time I give a speech, appear on Fox News, or write a column, I get positive feedback, but lots of negative feedback too. Just like FreedomWorks and other members of Project 21, I'm targeted because I'm simply expressing my views about ObamaCare, climate change legislation, the Second Amendment, and pro-growth economics. But along with the nasty comments, they also drag race into the discussion. I'd be happy to have negative email discussing the issues.

Every time we protest something Obama's done, we're labeled "racist"—because he's black. How can the left be okay with dropping race into every criticism of our commander in chief, on issues that have nothing to do with race whatsoever?

I still don't get how I'm considered a racist!

Racism is not the only accusation being hurled at Tea Partiers. We're called extremists too. FreedomWorks countered those claims with a website called "Stop the Haters" that highlights the critics' smear campaign.

There have been some dirty tricks like when the *former* voice-over talent for Geico Insurance, Lance Baxter aka D. C. Douglas, left hostile telephone messages at Freedom-Works' headquarters calling all of us "mentally retarded" and potential killers. Well, this guy was fired for his actions after we made the comments public.

FEW BLACKS INVOLVED

It's not surprising that only a few blacks are Tea Partiers.

About 95 percent of blacks voted for Obama during the presidential election and blacks have ethnic pride for having our nation's first black president. In addition, blacks overwhelmingly vote Democratic.

Now, with that as a background, why would you expect to find blacks at Tea Party rallies? After all, Tea Party rallies are critical of Obama's policies, and by definition the Tea Party's criticisms are messages that don't appeal to the vast majority of blacks. Furthermore, blacks who share Tea Party views about limited government are likely to remain silent to avoid alienation from friends, family, and coworkers. I know this from the e-mails I get from young people and others who are grateful I'm willing to speak up.

Of course, this does not mean more blacks will not become part of the movement. It's going to take some time for them to wake up and it can happen. If I woke up anyone can.

The rise in conservative blacks running for office is part of a growing blacklash against Obama's policies. Over time this will help liberate those who are chained to progressive dogma.

Having more conservative blacks as political role models is crucial for getting a greater percentage of minorities to think for themselves and avoid the traditional black leaders such as Jesse Jackson and Al Sharpton.

Look, even black politicians take a beating for not siding with Obama. Jesse Jackson slammed Representative Artur Davis, a Democrat from Alabama, saying, "You can't vote against health care and call yourself a black man." Jackson's statement was divisive.

Declining to respond in kind, Representative Davis said in a statement, "The best way to honor Reverend Jackson's legacy is to decline to engage in an argument with him that begins and ends with race."

Jesse Jackson should be ashamed for using the race card in that way in an attempt to influence the views of another black politician. It's embarrassing and goes against everything Americans stand for in this country—democracy, freedom of speech and expression, and the list goes on.

As per usual, Jackson was acting like a slave owner trying to keep blacks on his ideological plantation, where we are required to support government programs that increase public dependency on a bureaucracy. In Jackson's world, it appears a black man cannot have independent thought. He must follow Jackson blindly or face lashes from his tongue.

Listen up, all of you who have said that not getting behind big spending means you're a racist (and yes, that means you Jimmy Carter, Maureen Dowd, and many others):

You are crossing a very dangerous line with such accusations. The fact remains that the public is outraged about the president's policies—the spending, the budget, and the deficit—not his skin color. Period. Put any other notion to rest now.

President Obama was not elected only with black votes. Are those who cry racism saying the American people suddenly woke up and said, "Oh, he's black, so I don't like him anymore"? That makes no sense. The criticism of Obama's policies is about the policies—the stimulus, the growth of government, cap-and-trade, the health care bill, and the overspending.

But it's easier for the left to play the race card than address the public's legitimate concerns, but what the left and the media are doing is damaging and dangerous.

It's damaging because when everything is racist, then nothing is. Those who cry racism without evidence will cause people to tune out from cases in which there is evidence.

It's also dangerous to send a message that racism is behind everything. What does that tell young black men and women? It tells them they will never get a fair shake and that white people whom they have never met dislike them. With a message like that, it's no surprise we're seeing apparently racial incidents like the widely circulated September 2009 video of a young white student being beaten up on an Illinois school bus by black students while other black students cheer. What message have those black students internalized—that white people are their enemy?

If this continues the left will be responsible because it was too dishonest and too cowardly to have a fair debate with the American people on policy.

CONCLUSION

Uprising on the Plantation

Our country does not guarantee you success—but liberty guarantees you the opportunity to succeed.

—*Deneen Borelli*

I thought getting delayed when the buckles on my shoes set off the metal detector was the most drama I'd experience on May 25, 2011. But the fireworks had only just begun.

That was the day that all of my years of hard work and experience paid off. That's the day I sent myself a little mental note that read, "One person can make a difference." That's the day I confirmed for myself that what I do is important and that I'm speaking and writing and protesting and being an advocate because I believe in America and liberty and the people of this nation. I am doing it all and I'm representing the people while I'm doing it. May 25 was confirmation.

This is the part in my book—after you've heard all the things I am frustrated with in this country—where I show how we can and are making a difference. The Tea Party, National Center for Public Policy Research, Project 21, and FreedomWorks—we're changing things. We're fixing the way this country does business. We're making it better. One step at a time. And the message you should take from this: You can be a part of this movement too. You can make a difference too.

On that day in May, I had the opportunity to testify before the full U.S. House of Representatives Committee on Natural Resources about the inordinate financial hardship that Obama's war on fossil fuels imposes on poor and middle-class American households. (My testimony appears in Appendix 1.)

Me. Former model, track star, and kid from a regular family. The first person in my family to graduate from college. I was testifying in our nation's Capitol. My congressional testimony was presented as part of the "Harnessing American Resources to Create Jobs and Address Rising Gasoline Prices—Part III: Impacts on Seniors, Working Families and Memorial Day Vacations" oversight hearing. I considered this day a culmination of all my ambition and I drew upon my work as a shareholder advocate to ensure I made an impact.

I like to call my transition from political agnostic to activist an evolution, not a revolution. I had very little interest in politics and now I'm a very visible spokesperson for liberty. When you are finished reading my book I want you to know and believe I'm not just a talker. I'm taking action. I'm challenging the people I think are looting us of liberty and working very hard to keep us on the government plantation. I'm not just ending the book by writing about all of these characters and CEOs partnering with the president. I have gone head-to-head with these guys.

I will back up a little at this point because I want to share with you the path of advocacy that landed me in front of that panel in Washington that day in May.

In 2005, my husband, Tom, cofounded the Free Enterprise Action Fund—a shareholder activist mutual fund that used its shareholder standing to challenge progressive CEOs and their business strategies. In addition to selling the fund to investors, Tom did the trading and attended the majority of shareholder meetings for the fund, where he presented shareholder proposals and aggressively confronted CEOs about the basis of their decisions. I cut my teeth in shareholder activism initially by attending some meetings with Tom as part of his role as a portfolio manager. Over time, I moved from a spectator at shareholder meetings to an outright activist. My goal: to challenge CEOs who built business strategies on the growth of government, such as trying to profit from cap-and-trade legislation or in other cases where the CEO's personal agenda interfered with sound business practices. After the market crashed in 2008, the Free Enterprise Action Fund merged with another mutual fund and Tom left the financial services industry. However, Tom is continuing his shareholder activism work at the National Center for Public Policy Research, where he serves as director of the Free Enterprise Project.

I dipped my toes into challenging crony capitalism alongside Tom very early on, before it was all the rage. I was green when I began, but as I reflect on the successes and the impact we've made on the corporate landscape, I can really say the challenge has been worth the effort.

Facing CEOs on their home turf was challenging but truly rewarding. One of my first efforts in challenging a chief executive was in 2007 when I took on then–Caterpillar CEO Jim Owens over his support of cap-and-trade legislation during the company's annual shareholder meeting. From our perspective, a CEO selling to the construction industry shouldn't lobby for legislation that would raise energy prices, as this would have a negative impact on the construction industry. It doesn't make any business sense. He was shooting his industry in the foot.

So at the meeting, where he was surrounded by the support of both shareholders and employees, I asked a simple question: Did you do a cost-benefit analysis regarding the impact of cap-and-trade on your business? He tried ducking the question but I persisted—and guess what? Eventually he said no. So here's a major corporation, blindly lobbying for legislation that would change the nation, without having run the numbers on the impact the effort would have on the company's bottom line. Amazing. It was gratifying for me because I was able to drag the truth out of him. I was able to expose the recklessness of his lobbying efforts.

We continued our campaign against companies lobbying for cap-and-trade in 2010, when Tom and I attended the John Deere shareholder meeting. It was a very cold day in February in Moline, Illinois, as I recall, and once again we found ourselves in the middle of enemy territory—the meeting was at the company's headquarters and it was the first meeting for the company's new CEO, Samuel Allen. The same paradox existed with this company too: Deere was part of a lobbying coalition pursuing cap-and-trade, despite the fact that its customers in the agriculture industry were opposed to the legislation. So I challenged Allen about the company's support of the legislation and I expressed my concern that the company was contributing to a green bubble.

After the meeting the National Center for Public Policy Research—our employers—initiated an advertising campaign in partnership with FreedomWorks, which I also serve as a Fellow. We ran cable TV ads in cities where Deere is headquartered and where the company manufactures its products. The ad urged employees to call Deere's Human Resources Department hotline regarding the company's support of legislation that could result in their jobs being shipped overseas.

In the wake of our ad campaign, Deere decided to leave the United States Climate Action Partnership—the coalition lobbying for cap-and-trade. Caterpillar left it in 2009 after it discovered the Waxman-Markey cap-and-trade bill was going to harm its business. Gee—what a shocker!

Fresh off those victories, our biggest target was still GE CEO Jeff Immelt—Obama's partner and the king of crony capitalism. Challenging Immelt has now become almost a yearly affair for me. In 2009 in Orlando, Florida, Tom and I played a critical role in the shareholder meeting and generated national news coverage of it. We weren't the only ones frustrated. A number of shareholders challenged Immelt on a variety of issues, including the sagging stock price, Immelt's enduring support of cap-and-trade, constant concerns about MSNBC hurting GE's image, and the selling of infrastructure equipment to Iran. When I got my chance at the microphone I asked Immelt about news stories that claimed he tried to silence his business network CNBC's criticism of President Obama. At some point during our dialogue my microphone was cut off—talk about silencing! The incident made national news and was posted on the *Drudge Report.*

During the 2011 GE shareholder meeting we had one of our biggest successes of all. The National Center partnered with FreedomWorks again, this time on a public opinion poll of conservative voters about the favorability of General Electric and Johnson & Johnson—two companies that are supportive of Obama's policy objectives. GE's favorability plummeted from 51 percent to 20 percent when the respondents heard of the company's support of the Obama agenda.[1]

Armed with that information and the fact that petroleum company ConocoPhillips' CEO Jim Mulva was a GE board member, we traveled to Salt Lake City, Utah, in May 2011 to attend the meeting. Before it, though, we participated in the protest against crony capitalism and then we carried our activism inside the meeting. Tom and I were joined that day by David Ridenour, the vice president of the National Center, and by Kristina Ribali, FreedomWorks' media campaign coordinator.

Ridenour asked Immelt about the potential conflict of interest posed by Immelt's role as chairman of President Obama's Council on Jobs and Competitiveness while he simultaneously serves as CEO of GE. Tom, using our poll as ammunition, asked Immelt about the reputational risk for the company because GE is so aligned with Obama and his policies. It was Ribali's first shareholder meeting and she sarcastically congratulated Immelt for doing something amazing—Immelt's ability to unify the political left and right in opposition to his performance as CEO. In 2011, MoveOn.org launched a campaign to have Immelt removed from Obama's jobs panel because GE did not pay any taxes in 2010. That day I asked Immelt if his support for pricing carbon—that is, making fossil fuel prices more expensive through legislation—had the full support of his board of directors. Since Immelt danced around my question I remained persistent and he said he had the full support of the board. I quickly followed up by asking about Mulva's support since taxing carbon would be bad for his business, a fact that would also be true for another board member, James Tisch, president and CEO of Loews Corporation, which owns a large stake of Diamond Offshore Drilling, Inc., one of the largest offshore oil drilling companies in the world.

Immelt did not back down about having board support.

Well, a few days later during a speech at MIT Immelt said he had "lost interest in calling on the United States to develop a more comprehensive energy policy."² Additionally, a Reuters story said, "His [Immelt's] prior calls that the nation adopt regulations that put a price on carbon raised the hackles of some shareholders."³

Immelt's comment suggests he is backing off of his plan to push for cap-and-trade legislation. While we may never know why he felt the need to back off, I have a feeling that following the shareholder meeting, a few board members might have challenged Immelt, because of his effort to raise the price that would reduce demand for their fossil fuel products. We take his move as a sign of the success of our pressure that day.

So back to the big day in May, which was paved by my grassroots shareholder-activism work. I spoke of Obama's fossil fuel initiatives and how at odds I believe he is with the mood of American voters, the majority of whom think we should be drilling and mining more and developing our own gas, oil, and coal resources. Voters believe we're not doing enough as a nation to develop and become energy independent. The biggest crime, which I pointed out in my testimony, is that while the elites profit, the low- and fixed-income households pay a larger chunk of their household budget to energy. Simply put, it's a transfer of wealth—robbing the poor to pay the rich. For those families on the edge, this could push them to government dependency, which leads to more plantation politics.

I had prepared hard for that day of testimony. I opened by telling them, "In my work I promote the importance of limited government and personal responsibility as the key to personal success and social advancement." I had drafted my words carefully the weekend before and had Tom grill me because I knew questions would be challenging and I had to be ready. But honestly, the grilling at the dining room table was different from what I was about to experience that day.

Before I was up to speak, I tried to take the experience in. I was standing near the back of the room (which was nice by the way—my tax dollars at work) trying to focus on my surroundings, but I kept running my words through my head, prepping. Stepping into Room 1324 inside the Longworth House Office Building was a little like being in a Broadway theater awaiting the rising of the curtain. But this time, I was a part of the show.

I did take a moment to scan the room between being lost in my thoughts. I remember seeing Jon Runyan from New Jersey. "I know him," I thought to myself—he's the former offensive tackle drafted by the once Houston, now Tennessee, Titans and helped the team reach the Super Bowl in 2000. He also played with the Philadelphia Eagles, where he helped lead the team to a 2004 Super Bowl appearance. Like me, going from citizen to activist, he too had changed gears from NFL star to politician.

And then suddenly while I was lost in my thoughts—it was showtime. I opened the show as the first of four witnesses to testify. My testimony—full of facts—focused on President Obama's war on fossil fuels. I identified GE's Immelt as an elite who was going to be a winner of Obama's policy at the expense of hardworking Americans. And that's when sparks started flying.

It seemed obvious to me, but apparently not to Massachusetts Representative Ed Markey, that Immelt is in bed with Obama so he can walk away with profit. Plain and simple. But Markey started twisting the conversation and pounding me repeatedly with a question about my opinion on subsidies for big oil. Markey hammered me hard—repeating the same question over and over, but leaving little room for response. "Yes or no," he quipped, "Yes or no." Markey came at me—full assault—and didn't let me completely answer his question. He took the opportunity simply to grandstand and beat up on the oil industry, rambling on about subsidies to that sector. Mr. Markey— if you've listened to me at all, you'd know I'm anti-subsidy. I don't think the government should be giving money to any industry. That's a command-and-control strategy, which gives the government the power of the purse to pick winners and losers. Markey clouded the issue by redefining regular business tax deductions many companies get as subsidies.

What we really need is major tax reform that will eliminate special deals and the lobbyists who get paid to manipulate the tax code, but he really didn't care about an answer. He just wanted to steal the stage and quiet me, and the truth was revealing. And talk about a camera hog. It was drama.

I fielded many questions during the two-and-a-half-hour hearing—and in most other instances I was actually allowed to respond! Once the hearing was over, several Republican congressional members came over to me to shake my hand and told me I had done a great job. I have to tell you, I was motivated by the experience. I was moved by the fact that I was representing the thousands of Tea Party activists who have cheered me on during my rally speeches that challenged Obama's toxic energy policy. Ironically, I was the representative of the people; not all members of Congress that day can say the same.

While I really do see my day of testimony as a marker along the route of how far I've come, it's not the finish line in the race by any means. Life is a marathon, not a sprint, and the Tea Party, National Center for Public Policy Research, and FreedomWorks still have a lot of work to do. On our current path, this country is in trouble. Our government is spending too much money it does not have on things it does not do well—things like bailing out banks and running car companies that our Constitution doesn't even allow for. The left clamors for ever more taxes to pay for all these things without ever once asking: Does so much government actually work?

The Department of Energy was created to make our country energy independent. How's that working out? Since the creation of the federal Department of Education, the cost of government-run schools has skyrocketed while the basic reading and math skills of our children have consistently declined, particularly for black kids in inner-city schools. Welfare programs intended to be temporary help have locked poor Americans in a cycle of dependency. The Department of Housing and Urban Development, and Fannie Mae and Freddie Mac, were all complicit in a housing bubble that left many Americans paying mortgages they could not afford, or forced them into bankruptcy.

The list goes on and on. And on.

The answer is that much of our government does not work, it actually hurts people it claims to help, and it is putting a huge burden on our economy and our ability to grow and work as a nation. More worrisome is the current trend to use the government's Federal Reserve Bank to create new money and credit to paper over our addiction to spending and borrowing. That's a hidden tax on wage earners: folks like you and me who fill up our cars with gas to get to work and buy groceries to feed our families every week.

The men and women of the Tea Party say enough is enough! FreedomWorks' platform would be a good start to putting our road on the path to a "do-over." We need to shutter the government plantation, once and for all. Our nation's spending is out of hand and fiscally unsustainable. FreedomWorks and the National Center for Public Policy Research are intellectually grounded and helped me shape my views of liberty and limited government. I think their ideas could be the fix the country needs. I want to take you through some of them now.

BUDGET

If we hope to leave a legacy of opportunity and freedom to our children and grandchildren, the debt must stop here.

We need to put all failing "discretionary" spending on the chopping block. We simply can't afford it.

And that's just part of the solution. Numbers out of the Congressional Budget Office show a growing dependency of Americans on the government plantation when you compare stats from 1970 to 2010 and 2035. In 1970, 31 percent of the budget went to entitlements like Medicare, Medicaid, and Social Security. These are so-called mandatory programs that grow on autopilot regardless of our ability to pay the bills. By 2010, the share of budget spent on the entitlement programs had ballooned to 42 percent. Combine that $2.03 trillion spent on entitlements with the $209 billion spent on interest payments alone, and that is almost half of our 2010 budget. If that doesn't hurt you enough, projections for 2035 have us paying a whopping 25 percent in interest payments and a staggering 49 percent of our budget to entitlement spending. That means about 75 percent of our budget will be dedicated to entitlements and interest, leaving the remainder of our money going to discretionary funding such as defense and highways.[4]

Critical to our nation's success is rethinking entitlement spending. Long term, FreedomWorks proposes a real Balanced Budget Amendment to the U.S. Constitution that includes both a spending limitation and a supermajority for raising taxes, in addition to balancing revenues and expenses.[5] The best Balanced Budget Amendment legislation has been introduced by Tea Party freshman Senator Mike Lee of Utah, who replaced Republican Senator Robert

Bennett. He has already gotten the entire Republican Senate caucus to cosponsor this important reform.

The Tea Party has played a huge role in shifting the budget debate in Washington. The Tea Party's impact was seen during the debt ceiling debate in the summer of 2011. The government "right" of raising the debt level was transformed into a huge political debate. We are now focusing on spending cuts and a reduction in government services. The move is significant and due to the 2010 election, which was driven by the Tea Party movement. Medicare, Medicaid, and even Social Security spending are critical elements in the budget and debt battle. The public needs to be persuaded that these things can be run more efficiently without dramatic negative impact. It's possible.

TAX CODE

To achieve that limited government, we need to address not only our spending, but also our tax code. Freedom-Works advocates an initiative called "Scrap the Code," which points out the flaws of the current system. I agree our code is too big and too complex, and accordingly it's become an orgy of profit for tax lawyers and accountants who earn a living helping individuals and corporations avoid paying taxes.

The one and only purpose of the tax code is to raise the money to fund the legitimate role of government. But our code has become a politicized monster that attempts to socially engineer human behavior, with carve-outs and special treatment for politically favored special interests. In and of itself, the name of our tax code—a progressive tax—should have been a clue that it's doomed to fail. It's based on the notion that the more you make the more you should pay in taxes. The goal of the wealthy paying more than those who don't have wealth is not the problem—the trouble arises in how that goal is achieved. Without a doubt our current progressive tax system produces significant inequalities and distortions. For example, for the 2010 tax year almost half the country did not pay any federal income tax. My point here is not to create reverse class warfare of rich against poor—clearly, many wealthy individuals and corporations take advantage of the tax code to reduce their tax liabilities. My goal is simply to point out that our tax code is failing all of us.

The best system is a fair and simple one within which every citizen has some skin in the game. That's why I support the flat-rate tax system or flat tax. All taxpayers will pay the same flat rate. Here's how it works. The flat tax would replace the current burdensome tax system by simplifying the tax code with a single tax rate of about 17 percent. Almost all Americans except those making very little income would be paying into the system. In fact, many Eastern European countries including Russia are using a flat tax. Think of the additional costs savings that go into the process of taxes. A flat tax would essentially eliminate the IRS, and the huge fees from tax lawyers and accountants. Think of the economic productivity that could be generated if those great minds currently dedicated to avoiding paying taxes were focused on creating wealth through innovation and not loopholes designed by special interests.

I have to confess that I was sold on the flat tax when I was at CORE hosting our radio program, *The CORE Hour*, and I had the opportunity to interview Steve Forbes, who had just written his book *Flat Tax Revolution*. In addition to being an extremely nice and intelligent man, Forbes told our audience of the numerous advantages of the flat tax for our nation.[6]

OBAMACARE

FreedomWorks is clear on its position: repeal. Full repeal. The group is confident that with a GOP win in 2012, by 2013 ObamaCare will be a thing of the past. ObamaCare is not only a job killer for America, it will bankrupt the country. Costs will soar and the rationing of care will destroy the system. A patient-centered approach with choice is the only option.

FreedomWorks has a replacement solution though. First, participation in tax-subsidized plans will need to be both voluntary and portable. The playing field between what's offered from an employer and from individually purchased plans needs to be leveled. Second, high-risk pools need to be fully funded. Medicaid and Medicare pricing needs to come down and there needs to be both transparency and competition for each. And that's where choice comes in too: Medicare should be converted into a defined-contribution program with participation being voluntary. Price controls have to end for Medicare as well to reduce the rationing element. Another key replacement element: Health savings accounts should be promoted as a way to liberate families from government dependence. People should be able to control their choice and their spending on health care. Finally, states should be encouraged to lower costs and up competition through the reduction of competitive restrictions, malpractice reform, and mandated rating. The mantra that FreedomWorks hopes to use to generate enthusiasm is "Whose health care is it, anyway?"

One plan, proposed by Representative Jeff Flake, offers a bold alternative to the status quo, for both health care and our entitlement crisis: namely, personal ownership and control. His plan allows folks the option of saving their own hard-earned money currently taken in payroll taxes. Here's how that would work: People could choose to swap out their one-size-fits-all government retirement and Medicare health benefits for personal accounts and use this money to fund either need in retirement. This is what virtually all private sector companies have done by moving from a defined-benefit pension system to a defined-contribution system. These plans are portable and are controlled by the worker, not the company. You own it, you control it. The financial transition is the challenge, of course, because our government spends all of the payroll tax revenue that was supposedly being saved in a "trust fund." Maybe a phased-in program might be the best option for overcoming that hurdle.

The dirty secret is how unfair our bloated entitlement state is to blacks. Black men, in particular, pay payroll taxes into the government system their entire lives, but don't own or control those assets in retirement. Here's the problem: The average life expectancy of black men is about age sixty-nine—the same year Social Security and Medicare benefits kick in. So a life of "savings" disappears, spent by government on some other person or special interest. Real entitlement reform is based on freedom. It would allow every black man and woman to accumulate wealth that they control and could leave to their spouses and children when they pass away.

The left, of course, is adamantly opposed to such a plan. Makes you wonder what their real motive is, doesn't it? Here's a hint: It's about control and power.

THE ENVIRONMENT

FreedomWorks feels strongly that the regulatory zeal of the Environmental Protection Agency (EPA) needs to be curbed. Everyone wants a clean environment but the EPA's aggressive war against fossil fuels is harming economic growth and reducing the standard of living of Americans. Congress must step up and use its power to rein in the EPA. The agency's regulation of greenhouse gases must be stopped and the EPA's costly energy regulations of utility emissions must be dramatically scaled back. Too many of these regulations are being used as a weapon to reduce the use of fossil fuels without having a meaningful impact on health. Instead of the government restricting the development of our fossil fuel natural resources, we need a pro-growth energy policy that will allow the business community to invest in our country, keeping jobs in America, and generating much-needed tax revenue with the goal of making America an energy exporter—not an importer. Free markets, not crony capitalism, must dominate our economy. Failing CEOs like GE's Jeff Immelt should not be allowed to feed off the government and our tax dollars like a parasite and fuel government dependency by the rest of the country.

Who gets hit hardest by the high energy prices caused by radical environmentalism? Hardworking Americans and most of all low- and fixed-income households.

ARRIVING AT THE PODIUM

Frankly, I'm amazed at how I arrived at this point in my life. A nationally known figure who took significant risks getting to this point. After working in corporate America I found myself not knowing what my next career move should be.

But I wasn't the only risk taker in this venture.

Giovanna Cugnasca, a friend, introduced me to Niger Innis, spokesman for the Congress of Racial Equality, one of the oldest civil rights organizations. I volunteered my time learning about public policy as producer and cohost of the organization's weekly Internet radio talk show, *The CORE Hour*. Being involved with the talk show helped me learn and understand the issues so that I could discuss them on air live.

My experiences at CORE led to an opportunity to get involved with Project 21, an initiative of the National Center for Public Policy Research. Amy and David Ridenour, president and vice president, respectively, took a chance by hiring me as a full-time Project 21 Fellow. Part of the arrangement was for me to fund-raise for my fellowship—an activity I'm still executing. My concern early on was, who would give money to someone who is unknown and inexperienced?

My anxiety over fund-raising was quickly diminished while attending a Cato Institute event in Arizona. I had the pleasure of meeting a gentleman from California who was very intrigued with me and my personal story. I explained to him my new role with Project 21 and that I had to fund-raise for my salary and the very next day, he presented me with a personal check for one thousand dollars. My first donation! I wish all fund-raising were as easy as my first donor was. The nonprofit world is very competitive and it is difficult to fund-raise, especially when I spend most of my time engaged in activism. I've been extremely fortunate to have support from a very small—you can count them on one hand—but generous donors. Even to this day my salary at Project 21 is about 20 percent less than what I was making at Philip Morris in 2004.

Another concern I had as a Fellow was that one of my roles involved writing commentaries, and I must admit that in the beginning I was very intimidated with that part of the job. Coming from the corporate world, the most

I had written at length were memos, letters, and e-mails, not eight-hundred-plus words for a commentary! What I learned was that the more I wrote the better I got. To date, I have written numerous commentaries that have been published in major newspapers across the country. And, well, you're reading what's come out of that experience.

President and CEO of FreedomWorks Matt Kibbe and his team took a tremendous risk in putting together the 9/12 March on Washington DC in 2009. At that time, the prevailing wisdom was that "conservatives" don't do rallies—that's something the left does. Yet, despite this great uncertainty, FreedomWorks took a big leap and organized, partnering with dozens of other Tea Party leaders, the overwhelmingly successful 9/12 rally, which can easily be considered the conservative Woodstock.

FreedomWorks is now recognized as a leader in supporting, facilitating, and educating local Tea Party leaders all over the country.

In addition to not knowing if anyone would show up, FreedomWorks took another risk—they asked ME to be a prime-time speaker. I've known the FreedomWorks team for years and they are familiar with my views through my commentaries but they never heard me give a speech, especially before a crowd of almost a million people. Heck, the biggest crowd I addressed prior to this monumental day was probably no more than a hundred people!

One Friday evening in 2009 I was contacted by Terry Kibbe (Matt's wife) to see if I would be interested in speaking at their upcoming rally. I didn't give the offer a second thought. I was all in. What the heck, you only live once!

I wrote the speech a week before and prepared for the event at a friend's apartment using an ironing board as a podium, trying to visualize the possible surroundings and how I would deliver my speech the next day.

The night before the rally Tom and I had a sense that something big was up. We noticed cars and buses from around the country and there was that buzz in the air that something big was happening. It's the same feeling you get before a huge sporting event, whether it's a Stanley Cup Finals game or a college football national championship game—there's a lot of energy, excitement, and enthusiasm. My thoughts were validated driving from my friend's apartment in Virginia into the District early in the morning on September 12, 2009. Turns out we left just in time. As we pulled into Union Station to park, buses were rolling in so fast that it took a few minutes to get through the lot. Teems of people were walking around in their patriotic attire. T-shirts, head scarves, banners, flags, and everyone was friendly and smiling—just glad to be in the mix.

We took the short walk over to the Capitol, where we faced our biggest challenge. We didn't have our credentials to gain access to the stage. There was a momentary panic about what would happen if I couldn't get to the stage. So we took a chance by walking through the crowds, trying to find our way toward the front. As fate and luck would have it, we ran into Wayne Brough of FreedomWorks and a board member of the organization, C. Boyden Gray, who had credentials, making their way through the crowd. There were so many people sitting on lawn chairs or blankets and standing around waiting for something, anything, to happen. Happily, the crowd was very helpful and accommodating. All I had to say was that I was a speaker and like the scene in the movie *The Ten Commandments*, the crowds parted and we were on our way.

This major rally was the largest audience I ever spoke to before and was my introduction to patriotic Americans. God was with me that day. I delivered the speech of my life, which I have included in Appendix 2. I'm certainly no introvert, but people who know me know that my demeanor is calm and poised—after all, I was trained as a runway model. However, that day I had the passion of a Baptist minister. One of the opening lines I shouted during my speech, "We the People have had enough," resounded throughout the crowd and is featured in several inspirational YouTube clips and in the movie *Fire from the Heartland*, a documentary about conservative women in which I'm interviewed. Even family members were shocked and surprised at my delivery. My sister who was watching the event on television sent me a text after I spoke saying, "I barely recognized you! Where did that come from?" Some of the FreedomWorks staff whom I've known for years were also surprised.

The bold idea to give me a speaking opportunity that day and indeed the idea of the 9/12 rally was born from Brendan Steinhauser, a staffer at FreedomWorks. Brendan has long studied the left and he felt the political momentum surging to the right. I really felt that momentum that day.

Just before the event was closing out, we decided to get a head start out of the crowd. Being a veteran of football games at the old Giants Stadium, I'm very familiar with crowds and beating traffic. At this point in the day, I witnessed the most amazing experience of my life. For crowd-control purposes, Tom and I had to walk through areas that were fenced off, separating the crowd from the stage area. While walking past throngs of people—young, old, and from all over the country—I received an overwhelmingly amazing response. People were waving, screaming for me to come over to them to take pictures with me. They wanted to shake my hand and thank me for my bravery for taking on black leaders who are failing America. I signed autographs. There were hugs and kisses from these smiling patriots. There were tears. They thanked me for my message. It was a real rock star moment. I even got a marriage proposal! So much for claims of racism in the Tea Party movement. Fortunately, Tom caught this moment on video and to this day I still watch it with tears in my eyes.

A sound bite of my speech was included in the NBC News' coverage of the 9/12 rally and the following week I was interviewed on MSNBC and on Fox News' *Your World with Neil Cavuto*. My appearance on Cavuto led to a meeting with Fox News Channel Chairman and CEO Roger Ailes. Mr. Ailes, like many before him, took a risk with me and signed me on as a Fox News contributor. Prior to that week, I really had not participated in that many television interviews and when I did it was on the local news channels. My involvement with Fox News has been an amazing and rewarding experience.

Clearly, my evolution from a corporate employee to a nationally recognized figure demonstrates that the United States of America is truly an exceptional country, where if you're persistent, there will be people who will support you in many different capacities as long as you are willing to first help yourself.

MAKE A DIFFERENCE

I truly believe the people joining forces with the Tea Party movement have one huge thing in common that makes the movement a success: They are trying. They are simply trying to look at politics and the country with a fresh set of eyes. They are generating enthusiasm from otherwise non–politically active people because they are bringing new ideas into the fold. They are hoping to make the country a better place to live. And you know, they're succeeding. You can succeed by trying too.

It's not easy, don't get me wrong. Life, as I mentioned above, is like a marathon—only a few people run a marathon because it's work—true, legitimate work. A marathon requires a strong mind and body. Anyone considering running one needs stamina, endurance, and a clear set of goals. The same applies to life. We need to take small steps to accomplish large goals. That's what grassroots activism is about, but that is also what success in general is all about.

Get involved, take care of yourself, work hard, and you'll succeed at making a difference. At the very least, just try. Try to step out of that place in life that you feel isn't right for you. Try to speak your mind or be a force in your community. Try to better yourself because nobody is going to do it for you. I did. The way I see it, we all have the obligation to stand tall and fight for liberty. We are standing on the shoulders of untold numbers of military heroes who fought and died so that we can enjoy our freedom that, unfortunately, too many take for granted. Anyone who has served in the military, or is currently serving, deserves not only our thanks and respect but also a commitment from us to do our part to ensure their efforts were not in vain. I'm often moved and inspired by reading about and watching World War II movies about the sacrifices made by the greatest generation and I'm awed at the courage everyday Americans showed to preserve liberty. The best trip Tom and I ever took was to Normandy, France, touring the invasion beaches on the French coast in 2001, a month before September 11th. Being on Omaha and Utah Beaches, walking through the Normandy American Cemetery and Memorial, viewing the height of Pointe du Hoc, reading about the many battles at the various museums in the various towns in the region, was truly an amazing experience. The ingenuity and bravery of those men were awesome.

Thinking of what they did and what others have done in Iraq, Afghanistan, and everywhere else keeps my challenges in perspective. Would I rather be a paratrooper jumping behind enemy lines, running out of a landing craft, walking through a Middle Eastern desert, or waking up at 4:00 a.m. to debate a progressive political operative?

Easy choice, right?

I'm committed to using my God-given talents to fight for liberty so the next generation will have every opportunity to pursue their life, liberty, and pursuit of happiness.

APPENDIX 1

Congressional Testimony

Deneen Borelli
Project 21 Fellow
National Center for Public Policy Research

*"Harnessing American Resources to Create Jobs and
Address Rising Gasoline Prices—Part III: Impacts on
Seniors, Working Families and Memorial Day Vacations"*

MAY 25, 2011

Thank you for the opportunity to testify today.

My name is Deneen Borelli. I'm a full-time Fellow with Project 21, a black conservative public policy group; a Fellow with FreedomWorks and a Daily Caller columnist. In my work I promote the importance of limited government and personal responsibility as the key to personal success and social advancement.

Sadly, our country's natural resources are under assault

by environmentalists, business interests and progressive politicians. Their plan is to raise the price of fossil fuels to make renewable energy sources more economically competitive.

This is a bad plan for our economy, jobs and hardworking Americans.

Affordable energy is the life blood of our economy and, consequently, a primary driver of the quality of life for all Americans.

Today many Americans are facing significant financial difficulties due to soaring energy costs. Skyrocketing gasoline prices are especially burdensome for hardworking American families whose budgets are also being squeezed from rising food prices.

According to AAA's Fuel Gauge Survey, the national average of self-serve regular gasoline is about $3.886—that is about double the price per gallon at $1.838 when President Obama was sworn into office.

Recent public opinion polls and news stories have documented the impact of rising energy prices on Americans. A recent *USA Today*/Gallup Poll found 7 in 10 Americans said high gasoline prices are bringing about financial hardships for them and just over 20 percent said their standard of living is in danger because of the higher prices at the pump.

A *Washington Post*/ABC poll in April also found that 7 in 10 said their families were suffering financial hardships because of high gasoline prices.

Naturally, middle- and lower-income families are hardest hit by soaring energy prices. A study prepared by

Eugene M. Trisko, Esquire, on behalf of the American Coalition of Clean Coal Electricity concluded that:

- Lower-income households are paying nearly a quarter of their income for energy costs. The 27 million lower-income households earning between $10,000 and $30,000, representing 23% of U.S. households, will allocate 23% of their 2011 after-tax income to energy, more than twice the national average of 11%.

- Household gasoline costs have more than doubled in the past ten years, from an average of $1,680 in 2001 to a projected $3,601 in 2011. Increased gasoline costs account for 75% of the $2,562 average household energy cost increase since 2001.

- Minority households are disproportionately impacted by higher energy costs. In 2009, 62% of Hispanic households and 67% of black households had average annual incomes below $50,000, compared with 46% of white households and 39% of Asian households. Energy costs represent a much larger fraction of disposable income for households earning less than $50,000 than for wealthier families. Due to these income inequalities, the burdens of energy price increases are imposed disproportionately on black and Hispanic households.

CNNMoney recently reported that the average American household spent about $368 on fuel in April. That amount is more than twice what U.S. households spent two years ago and it represents about 9 percent of their total monthly income.

The sobering poll and economic data predicted from high energy prices referenced above is now reverberating through our economy. Wal-Mart, the nation's largest retailer, and Lowe's, a home improvement chain, cited higher gasoline prices as the cause of disappointing sales. Both companies said consumer traffic was down in their stores.

Big retailers are not the only casualty of high gas prices. According to a poll by DollarDays.com, a wholesale distributor, more than 64 percent of small business owners attribute high gas prices to a drop in revenue and more than 25 percent are concerned they will have to lay off workers if prices stay high.

The impact of high gas prices on disposable income was summarized by an economist for the National Federation of Independent Businesses, "If all your customers are paying $50 for a tank of gas that they used to pay $25 for, somebody is not getting that $25."

With unemployment hovering at 9 percent and economic growth sluggish, our country can't afford to have the high costs of energy put our economy in reverse.

Tragically, President Obama's energy policy is contributing to the economic pain being experienced by hardworking American families. Instead of having a policy that would take advantage of our abundant supply of domestic natural resources—coal, oil and natural gas, which

currently provide about 85 percent of our energy needs—
the President is waging a war on fossil fuels.

The President's energy policy is to discourage the use of
fossil fuels through regulations that raise the cost of their
use and to reduce supply by blocking natural resource exploration and extraction.

Disturbingly, this dual strategy will indeed make energy prices "skyrocket" while stifling economic growth,
driving jobs overseas.

By forcing the cost of traditional forms of energy
higher, President Obama wants to make renewable energy
sources cost competitive. It's a command-and-control energy policy where the federal government takes an active
role in picking energy winners and losers.

Instead of adopting an energy policy that takes advantage of the reliability, affordability and availability of fossil
fuel based energy, the President is advancing a renewable
energy strategy that includes generating 80 percent of electricity from clean energy sources by 2035.

The winners in President Obama's energy policy are the
well-connected corporate and social elite while the losers
are the hardworking Americans who will have to suffer
the economic consequences of higher energy prices, slower
economic growth and jobs moving overseas.

It's fundamentally a wealth transfer mechanism from
the middle- and lower-income households to the pockets
of corporate heads and billionaire investors who want to
profit from renewable energy.

The President's hostility toward fossil fuels is well documented.

While running for President, then-Senator Obama said his cap-and-trade energy policy would make electricity prices "necessarily skyrocket" and it would "bankrupt" power plants that use coal as an energy source.

The goal of higher energy prices is also shared by Energy Secretary Steven Chu. In 2008, Secretary Chu said, "Somehow we have to figure out how to boost the price of gasoline to the levels in Europe."

After cap-and-trade failed to pass in the Senate, President Obama merely shifted gears to reassert his anti-fossil fuel agenda through the executive branch. In an interview with *Rolling Stone* magazine last September, President Obama said, "One of my top priorities next year is to have an energy policy that begins to address all facets of our overreliance on fossil fuels. We may end up having to do it in chunks, as opposed to some sort of comprehensive omnibus legislation."

Delivering on his promise to execute his agenda in "chunks," President Obama is wielding his executive powers to discourage the use of fossil fuels by allowing the EPA to regulate greenhouse gas emissions under the Clean Air Act.

By cracking down on emissions such as carbon dioxide, which is released when fossil fuels are burned, EPA regulations would raise the price of energy with a particularly devastating effect on coal-fired electricity generation. Coal is a cheap and abundant natural resource that currently provides about half of our country's electricity.

The Obama Administration is also impeding the ability of energy companies to develop our country's natural resources.

Following the deepwater drilling moratorium in the Gulf of Mexico, the approval process for drilling permits has been extremely slow. It took four months for the first drilling permit to be approved following the end of the moratorium and the rate of approvals remains unacceptably slow.

The reduction in oil production as a result of the Obama Administration cracking down on drilling permits is significant. According to the Energy Information Administration, the decrease in domestic production this year was estimated to be about 200,000 barrels per day and that production falloff is expected to continue through 2012.

As a result of the uncertainty surrounding the drilling approvals, seven deepwater rigs have left the Gulf of Mexico and with them a number of high paying jobs.

The Obama Administration's assault on oil drilling is not restricted to the Gulf of Mexico. The EPA recently refused to issue air permits to allow Shell Oil Company to continue with an exploration project off the northern coast of Alaska. The company has spent about $4 billion in leases and exploration costs in an effort to produce an estimated 27 billion barrels of oil.

The EPA's hostility towards fossil fuel development is not restricted to oil production. The agency's approval of coal mining permits is extremely slow, and, in unprecedented action, the EPA revoked a mining permit for Arch Coal after it had been issued. The company said the EPA's action would block an estimated $250 million investment in the project that would have created 250 jobs.

Unfortunately, President Obama's dislike of fossil fuels is restricted only to our country. While in Brazil in March, Obama promoted an offshore drilling project in Brazil for which, he said, the U.S. would ". . . be one of your best customers" and ". . . the United States could not be happier with the potential for a new, stable source of energy."

Clearly, "We the People" would be much happier if our President would allow us to have the same opportunity to develop the natural resources in the U.S. and not in Brazil.

To lower energy costs for all Americans, grow our economy and become energy independent, we need a new energy policy that will encourage the development of our own natural resources.

According to the Congressional Research Service (CRS), the U.S. has more abundant sources of fossil fuels than any other country. The CRS reported:

- The U.S. has an estimated 163 billion barrels of recoverable oil.

- The U.S. has an estimated 2,047 trillion cubic feet of natural gas.

- The U.S. has an estimated 262 billion short tons of coal.

A study by Wood Mackenzie estimated the economic impact of giving the energy industry access to U.S. oil and natural gas resources that are currently unavailable. The study estimated that the industry would create 530,000 jobs and provide $150 billion in revenue (tax, royalty and other sources) to the government by 2025.

Just imagine the amount of economic growth that could be generated if the federal government had an energy policy that allowed industry to develop the stunning amount of natural resources cited in the CRS study.

Importantly, the American people support development of our natural resources.

According to Rasmussen Reports:

- 50 percent of adults believe the United States should produce more domestic oil by allowing drilling in the Arctic National Wildlife Refuge (ANWR);

- 67 percent now support offshore oil drilling, the highest level of support since the BP leak erupted in the Gulf of Mexico and;

- 76 percent of voters say the United States doesn't do enough to develop its own gas and oil resources.

Clearly, President Obama's anti-fossil fuel energy policy is on a collision course with the attitudes of the majority of Americans.

The President needs to shake loose from the corporate and environmental activist special interest groups that have influenced his policy and reverse course and adopt a pro-growth energy strategy.

There is something terribly wrong when the corporate and social elite can use the power of government to advance their narrow interests while harming the standard of living of hardworking Americans, denying us our right to "life, liberty and the pursuit of happiness."

Seventy-six percent of voters believe the U.S. is not doing enough to develop our own natural resources. The powerful few should not block the will of the people.

APPENDIX 2

FreedomWorks Rally Speech

What's up America!!

Let's set the record straight right now—we are here today because—"We the People have had enough." We will NOT sit silently while our liberties and freedoms are being looted by elected officials that are serving their interests while ignoring their constituents. We will NOT sit silently and let the massive growth of government smother our right to "Life, Liberty and the Pursuit of Happiness." We will NOT sit silently and let the massive growth of government debt crush our future and the future of our children. Our rally today is about liberty! Personally, I will NOT sit silently and allow our critics to say our cause is about race and that we are a bunch of red necks. Hey Janeane Garofalo—my neck isn't red!!!! Speaking of race—I am outraged that prominent black politicians who use the race card any chance they get to cover their failures and their failed policies.

I'm also stunned that black politicians have an affinity for socialism. Here are a few examples—

Charles Rangel Chairman of the House Ways & Means Committee says "bias" and "prejudice" against President Obama are the reasons why there's so much opposition to the health care proposal. Mr. Rangel, our opposition to ObamaCare is about policy not race. Mr. Rangel—just pay your taxes!!! Congressman John Conyers questioned the need for lawmakers to read the health care bill. Mr. Conyers—just read the bill!!! Congresswoman Diane Watson admires Fidel Castro and Congresswoman Maxine Waters supports government takeover and control of oil companies.

Congresswomen that's socialism and it's evil—it's a political philosophy that robs human dignity.

America just look at the condition of the urban communities these politicians represent.

Are the communities of Harlem, Detroit and Los Angeles any better since these individuals have been in office?

As a board member with the Opportunity Charter School in Harlem, New York, I can tell you that the government run schools are failing our children.

Not only have these liberal policies failed, they are trying to make matters much worse by supporting cap-and-trade.

Let's get the terminology straight. In Washington DC they call it cap-and-trade but in reality it's an energy tax!

The goal of cap-and-tax is to force Americans to use less energy by making it more expensive.

The consequences of higher energy prices will be devastating:

- it will reduce our disposable income and our standard of living;

- it will lead to job losses when manufacturing jobs move overseas;

- it will reduce economic growth.

That's why cap-and-tax is a ball and chain for all Americans but especially for low income households.

It's an energy policy that will enslave all of us.

For the sake of liberty and limited government—we cannot allow cap-and-tax to move in the Senate.

America—Emancipation from the race card, socialism and cap-and-tax will bring about the change all Americans can believe in.

God Bless You and God Bless America!

NOTES

INTRODUCTION: HARD WORK, NOT HANDOUTS

1. "Obama rips U.S. Constitution," http://www.wnd.com/ ?pageId=79225#ixzzlZjDvADaA.
2. Ibid.

CHAPTER ONE: THE GOOD OL' GOVERNMENT PLANTATION

1. http://www.politico.com/news/stories/0810/40533 .html.
2. http://www.usatoday.com/money/general/2002/03/25/ reparations-sidebar.htm.
3. http://nation.foxnews.com/jesse-jackson/2011/03/05/ wisconsin-capitol-jesse-jackson-compares-scott-walker -racist-democrat-georg#ixzz1IZaQpVZh.
4. http://www.progressive.org/wx0304b11.html.
5. http://www.realclearpolitics.com/video/2011/03/10/ jesse_jackson_in_wisconsin_were_going_to_escalate_ the_protests.html.
6. Peter Flaherty, "Fannie Mae and Freddie Mac Lavish Contributions on Jesse Jackson as Companies Melt

Down," National Legal Policy Center, July 14, 2008, http://www.nlpc.org/view.asp?action=viewArticle&aid =2603 as of August 7, 2008.

7. Ibid.

8. Joseph Shuman, "Housing and Budgets and Banks, Oh My," *Wall Street Journal*, July 23, 2008, http:// online.wsj.com/article/SB121679516878376785.html? apl=y&r=399234 as of August 7, 2008.

9. Peter Flaherty, "All in the Family: Anheuser-Busch Pays Off the Diversity Activists," National Legal Policy Center, February 10, 2006, http://www.nlpc.org/view.asp? action=viewArticle&aid=1263 as of August 7, 2008.

10. Peter Flaherty, "NLPC Asks Corporations to Stay Away from Jesse Jackson's Wall Street Conference; Ethics Group Cites Controversy, Anti-Semitism at Last Rainbow/PUSH Event," National Legal Policy Center, December 1, 2005, http://www.nlpc.org/view .asp?action=viewArticle&aid=1183 as of August 7, 2008.

11. Timmerman, Kenneth R., *Shakedown—Exposing the Real Jesse Jackson* (Washington, DC: Regnery Publishing, Inc., 2002), viii.

12. Ibid., 417.

13. Peter Flaherty, "Rev. Jesse Jackson and Peter Flaherty Discuss Rainbow/PUSH Wall Street Project," broadcast transcript, WTWP-FM, Washington, DC, National Legal Policy Center, October 24, 2006, http://www.nlpc.org/view.asp?action=viewArticle&aid =1750 as of August 7, 2008.

14. Timmerman, *Shakedown,* 291–92.

16. Charles Gasparino, *King of the Club: Richard Grasso and the Survival of the New York Stock Exchange* (New York: HarperCollins, 2007), 115–16.

17. Ibid.

18. William Claiborne, "Jackson's Fundraising Methods Spur Questions," *Washington Post*, March 27, 2001, available at http://www.lexis.com/research/retrieve?_m=663a42ce8f40cc769a6e5ff14819ade3&docnum=2&_fmtstr=FULL&_startdoc=1&wchp=dGLbVzb-zSkAb&_md5=d420fdca812ef53b00bb2ff213b40b37&focBudTerms=jesse%20jackson%20and%20The%20Washington%20Post%20and%20William%20Claiborne&focBudSel=all (accessed August 7, 2008).

19. Ibid.

20. Jeffrey H. Birnbaum, "Radio Merger Under Fire from Black Lawmakers; Caucus, FCC Chair Differ on Setting Aside XM, Sirius Channels for Minorities," *Washington Post*, June 17, 2008, available at http://www.lexis.com/research/retrieve?_m=ca2cd1e20b8ac6a9302e6001aa234e25&docnum=4&_fmtstr=FULL&_startdoc=1&wchp=dGLbVzW-zSKAA&_md5=0e104aa137e17e4d4cd576f695a94f61&focBudTerms=Chester%20Davenport&focBudSel=all (accessed August 28, 2008).

21. Ibid.

22. Ryan Saghir, "Jesse Jackson, Chester Davenport Meet with FCC Commissioners," Orbitcast.com, http://

www.orbitcast.com/archives/jesse-jackson-chester
-davenport-meet-with-fcc-commissions.html (accessed
August 18, 2008).

23. Ibid.
24. http://www.nytimes.com/1999/04/12/business/
how-one-man-used-corporate-affirmative-action-in
-ameritech-deal.html?pagewanted=all&src=pm.
25. Federal Communications Commision, "Hearing Public Meeting, Washington, DC," October 31, 2007,
hearing transcript available at http://www.fcc.gov/
localism/dc_transcript.pdf (accessed August 18, 2008).
26. http://www.forbes.com/2008/07/25/fcc-approves-xm
-sirius-merger-tech-cx_pco_0725paidcontent.html.
27. "JPMorgan Chase Shareholders' Meeting, Q&A Session with CEO James Dimon, Questioners Jesse Jackson and Deneen Borelli," May 20, 2008, transcript
available at http://www.nationalcenter.org/JPMorgan
Transcript052008.pdf (accessed August 7, 2008).
28. Michael J. de la Merced, "Jackson Calls for Changes to
Visa I.P.O.," *New York Times*, March 5, 2008, http://
dealbook.blogs.nytimes.com/2008/03/05/a-call-for
-fairness-in-visas-ipo/?scp=2&sq=jesse%20jackson%20
jpm%20chase&st=cse (accessed August 18, 2008).
29. Ibid.
30. Ibid.
31. "JPMorgan Chase Shareholders' Meeting, Q&A Session with CEO James Dimon, Questioners Jesse Jackson and Deneen Borelli."

32. http://www.conservativeblog.org/amyridenour/
    2008/6/10/project-21s-borelli-rebuts-jesse-jackson-at
    -jpmorgan-chase-s.html.
33. http://en.wikipedia.org/wiki/Tawana_Brawley_rape_
    allegations.
34. http://www.nydailynews.com/news/2007/11/18/2007
    -11-18_20_years_later_tawana_brawley_has_turned
    .html.
35. http://www.washingtonpost.com/wp-dyn/content/
    article/2011/01/11/AR2011011104334.html.
36. http://en.wikipedia.org/wiki/Al_Sharpton.
37. http://thehill.com/blogs/hillicon-valley/technology/
    141419-al-shartpon-tells-fcc-to-keep-racism-off-the
    -air-in-light-of-tucson-shootings.
38. http://www.nytimes.com/2011/07/28/business/media/
    for-al-sharpton-questions-on-ties-to-comcast.html.
39. http://www.ktla.com/news/landing/ktla-arizona-immi
    gration-march,0,5422761.story.
40. http://www.nypost.com/p/news/local/sharpton_
    pledge_to_fight_ariz_immig_O7cdlDmQ5GwTBrq
    ZrorD5O#ixzz1DsL7yMOr.
41. http://www.nydailynews.com/news/politics/2011/04/
    06/2011-04-06_obama_looks_to_al_for_help_
    in_12_run.html?print=1&page=all.
42. Dana Milbank, "Charlie Rangel's Censure, House's
    Disgrace," *Washington Post,* December 4, 2010, avail-
    able at http://www.washingtonpost.com/wp-dyn/con
    tent/article/2010/12/03/AR2010120301911.html.

43. http://online.wsj.com/article/AP1934d01c855443b7a

43. http://online.wsj.com/article/AP1934d01c855443b7a
259b84ed43275a4.html.

44. http://www.washingtonpost.com/wp-dyn/content/
gallery/2011/01/31/GA2011013102096.html?hpid=top
news#photo=1.

45. http://www.nytimes.com/2008/07/11/nyregion/11
rangel.html.

46. http://www.politico.com/news/stories/1110/45198.html.

47. http://thehill.com/homenews/house/183047-house
-leaders-to-honor-rangel-nine-months-after-censure.

48. http://www.foxnews.com/politics/2009/09/03/rangel
-prejudice-obama-halting-health-care-reform/.

49. http://www.nydailynews.com/news/2009/08/21/
2009-08-21_gov_david_paterson_blames_call_for_
html.

50. http://michellemalkin.com/2009/08/28/race-baiter
-democrat-rep-diane-watson-praises-cuban-health
-system-castro-guevara-who-kicked- out-the-wealthy/.

CHAPTER TWO: THE OBAMA IRONY

1. http://online.wsj.com/article/SB122581133077197035
.html.

2. Jeffrey M. Jones, "Americans Less Likely to View
Obama as a Strong Leader," Gallup, March 30, 2011,
http://www.gallup.com/poll/146876/Americans-Less
-Likely-View-Obama-Strong-Leader.aspx.

3. Frank Newport, "D.C., Hawaii Still Most Approv-
ing of Obama; All States Decline," Gallup, February

23, 2011, http://www.gallup.com/poll/146294/Hawaii -Approving-Obama-States-Decline.aspx.

4. Frank Newport, "Six in 10 Say Obama Has Spent Too Little Time on Economy," Gallup, February 10, 2010, available at http://www.gallup.com/poll/125774/Six -Say-Obama-Spent-Little-Time-Economy.aspx.

5. http://dailycaller.com/2011/06/10/federal-data -shows-troubling-unemployment-underemployment -trends/.

6. http://www.washingtonpost.com/wp-dyn/content/ article/2010/08/12/AR2010081204918.html.

7. http://www.nytimes.com/2010/03/22/business/22 bizhealth.html?pagewanted=2&ref=policy.

8. http://www.moneyweek.com/investment-advice/ profit-from-us-healthcare-reform-01212.

9. http://webcache.googleusercontent.com/search?q= cache:2q_6JyVfnyMJ:transcripts.cnn.com/TRAN SCRIPTS/1101/02/sotu.01.html+one+trillion+dollar s+in+stimulus+that+went+to+bail+out+Wall+Street& cd=4&hl=en&ct=clnk&gl=us&client=firefox-a& source=www.google.com.

10. http://www.examiner.com/political-buzz-in-dallas/ sherman-black-panther-case-attacks-on-eric-holder -blacked-out-of-media-poll-video-transcript.

11. http://biggovernment.com/abreitbart/2011/10/03/ shock-photos-barack-obama-with-new-black-panther -party-on-campaign-trail-in-2007/.

12. http://www.huffingtonpost.com/2010/04/17/charles -ogletree-sharpton_n_541824.html.

13. Barack Obama, *The Audacity of Hope: Thoughts on Reclaiming the American Dream* (New York: Crown Publishers, 2006), 25.
14. Ibid.
15. Dinesh D'Souza, *The Roots of Obama's Rage* (Washington, DC: Regnery Publishing, Inc., 2010), 19.
16. http://www.telegraph.co.uk/news/worldnews/barack obama/4623148/Barack-Obama-sends-bust-of -Winston-Churchill-on-its-way-back-to-Britain.html.

CHAPTER THREE: DIGGING DEEP HOLES

1. The Heritage Foundation, "Married Fathers: America's Greatest Weapon Against Child Poverty," June 16, 2010, http://www.heritage.org/research/reports/2010/ 06/married-fathers-americas-greatest-weapon-against -child-poverty.
2. http://www.cdc.gov/nchs/data/nvsr/nvsr59/nvsr59_01 .pdf, 15.
3. http://www.msnbc.msn.com/id/39993685/ns/health -womens_health/.
4. http://www.time.com/time/magazine/article/ 0,9171,974473,00.html.
5. http://www.census.gov/hhes/www/poverty/about/ overview/index.html.
6. http://www.nytimes.com/2011/09/14/us/14census .html?pagewanted=all.
7. Robert Rector, Katherine Bradley, and Rachel Sheffield, "Obama to Spend $10.3 Trillion on Welfare: Uncovering the Full Cost of Means-Tested Welfare

or Aid to the Poor," Heritage Foundation, September 16, 2009, http://www.heritage.org/research/reports/2009/09/obama-to-spend-103-trillion-on-welfare-uncovering-the-full-cost-of-means-tested-welfare-or-aid-to-the-poor.

8. Heritage Special Report, September 16, 2009, published by the Heritage Foundation.

9. Charles Murray, *Losing Ground: American Social Policy, 1950–1980* (New York: Basic Books, 1994).

10. http://goliath.ecnext.com/coms2/gi_0199-5155969/Charles-Murray-Ending-Welfare-As.html.

11. Michael Barone, "Charles Murray, Abolish the Welfare State," *U.S. News & World Report,* March 29, 2006, http://www.usnews.com/opinion/blogs/barone/2006/03/29/charles-murray-abolish-the-welfare-state.

12. Charles Murray, *In Our Hands: A Plan to Replace the Welfare State* (Washington, DC: AEI Press, 2006).

13. Charles Murray, "A Plan to Replace the Welfare State," *Wall Street Journal,* March 22, 2006, reprinted by the American Enterprise Institute for Public Policy Research, available at http://www.aei.org/article/24092.

14. Walter Williams, quoted by Jason L. Riley, "The State Against Blacks," *Wall Street Journal,* January 22, 2011.

15. Walter Williams, *Up from the Projects: An Autobiography* (Stanford, Cal.: Hoover Institution Press, 2010).

16. http://online.wsj.com/article/SB10001424052748704881304576094221050061598.html.

17. Ibid.

18. http://www.jewishworldreview.com/cols/sowell042103.asp.

19. Peter S. Goodman, "From Welfare Shift in '96, a Reminder for Clinton," *New York Times,* April 11, 2008.
20. The Heritage Foundation, "Stimulus Bill Abolishes Welfare Reform and Adds New Welfare Spending," February 11, 2009, http://www.heritage.org/research/reports/2009/02/stimulus-bill-abolishes-welfare-reform-and-adds-new-welfare-spending.
21. "Number of Welfare Recipients Rises Sharply," truthdig, June 22, 2009, http://www.truthdig.com/eartotheground/item/20090622_number_of_welfare_recipients_rise_sharply/.
22. "Ending Welfare Reform as We Knew It," *National Review Online,* February 12, 2009, http://www.nationalreview.com/articles/226878/ending-welfare-reform-we-knew-it/editors.
23. Ibid.
24. "Welfare Rolls up in '09; More Enroll in Assistance Programs," *USA Today,* January 26, 2010, http://www.usatoday.com/news/nation/2010-01-25-welfare-rolls_N.htm.
25. "Record Number in Government Anti-Poverty Programs," *USA Today,* August 30, 2010, http://www.usatoday.com/news/washington/2010-08-30-1Asafetynet30_ST_N.htm.
26. Alan Bjerga, "Food Stamp Recipients at Record 41.8 Million Americans in July, U.S. Says," *Bloomberg,* October 5, 2010, http://www.bloomberg.com/news/2010-10-05/food-stamp-recipients-at-record-41-8-million-americans-in-july-u-s-says.html.

27. U.S. Department of Education, "Status Dropout Rates of 16 through 24-Year Olds in the Civilian, Noninstitutionalized Population, by Race/Ethnicity: Selected Years, 1980–2008," available from the National Center for Education Statistics at http://nces .ed.gov/fastfacts/display.asp?id=16.

28. "Obama Kids to Attend Private D.C. School," CBS News, November 21, 2008, http://www.cbsnews .com/stories/2008/11/21/politics/main4625929 .shtml.

29. http://www.nytimes.com/2010/03/02/us/02-obama .html.

30. Bob Ewing, "The Education Debacle of the Decade," *Daily Caller,* July 6, 2010, http://dailycaller.com/ 2010/07/06/the-education-debacle-of-the-decade/.

31. http://www.deneenborelli.com/commentaries/dont -waste-your-time-if-you-cant-pay-the-prime/.

32. "Homeowners to Banks: We Want to Be Home for the Holidays Too," request from the National Training and Information Center (NTIC), the NAACP and community groups from around the country on November 28, 2007. Available from the NTIC online at http://www.ntic-us.org/documents/Homeforthe HolidaysPressRelease_000.pdf.

33. See, for example, "H.R. 4135: Family Foreclosure Rescue Corporation Act, 2007–2008," at http://www .govtrack.us/congress/bill.xpd?bill=h110-4135.

34. Frédéric Bastiat, *The Law* (Minneapolis: Filiquarian Publishing, 2005), 7.

35. Michelle Caruso-Cabrera, *You Know I'm Right* (New York: Simon & Schuster, 2010), 66.
36. http://video.foxnews.com/v/4560891/beck-hiroshima -vs-detriot.
37. http://www.lohud.com/article/20111002/NEWS01/ 110020329/Condition-critical-New-Yorks-Medicaid -benefits-costliest-United-States.

CHAPTER FOUR: HOW BLACK LEADERS FAIL US

1. Bill Cosby, "Address at the NAACP on the 50th Anniversary of Brown v. Board of Education," delivered May 17, 2004, at Constitution Hall in Washington, DC. Available at American Rhetoric Online Speech Bank, http://www.americanrhetoric.com/speeches/bill cosbypoundcakespeech.htm.
2. RiShawn Biddle, "The Kids Can't Read," *American Spectator,* June 21, 2010, http://spectator.org/archives/ 2010/06/21/the-kids-cant-read.
3. Ibid.
4. http://www.parentdish.com/2011/01/21/cursive-hand writing/.
5. http://www.cypress.com/?rID=34981.
6. Aliyah Shahid, "McDonald's Beating Video: Victim Is Transgender, Maryland Attack is Hate Crime, Says Advocacy Group," *Daily News,* April 23, 2011, http:// articles.nydailynews.com/2011-04-23/news/29484 684_1_transgender-woman-advocacy-group-victim.
7. "Spaghetti Sparks Subway Fight (Video)," *New York Post,* March 18, 2011, http://www.nypost.com/p/

news/local/spaghetti_sparks_subway_fight_video_
uPovPjeHr94thJ0nj6HP6N.

8. Glenn Blain and Kenneth Lovett, "New York City
School Aid Sliced by Millions as Lawmakers Finalize
On-Time State Budget," *Daily News,* March 30, 2011,
http://articles.nydailynews.com/2011-03-30/local/
29381961_1_state-budget-school-aid-lawmakers.

9. "Teachers Union, NAACP Suing to Block School
Closings," NBC New York, February 1, 2010, http://
www.nbcnewyork.com/news/local/Teachers-Union
-NAACP-Suing-to-Block-School-Closings-83261162
.html, Lindsey Christ, "Officials: 47 Schools Considered for Closure," NY1, October 28, 2011, http://
origin.ny1.com/content/top_stories/127949/officials
-47-schools-considered-for-closure.

10. http://www.nytimes.com/2010/05/05/us/politics/
05blacks.html?_r=3&hp=pagewanted=print.

11. "Black Republicans Score Historic Inroads," Newsmax
.com, November 3, 2010, http://www.newsmax.com/
InsideCover/black-gop-wins-allan/2010/11/03/375950.

12. Fox News, *On the Record with Greta Van Susteren,*
November 19, 2011.

13. "Black Republican: Black Caucus Preaches Victimization And Dependency," *The Hill,* November 20, 2010,
http://thehill.com/blogs/blog-briefing-room/news/
130237-black-republican-congressional-black-caucus
-preaches-victimization-and-dependency.

14. http://www.nydailynews.com/news/national/2010/07/
31/2010-07-31_rep_maxine_waters_to_be_charged_
with_ethics_violations.html#ixzz1Ecb1ahN2.

15. http://weaselzippers.us/2010/12/25/reprobate-john
-conyers-reimburses-govt-for-sons-use-of-govt-vehicle/.
16. http://www.sourcewatch.org/index.php?title=House_
Ethics_Committee.
17. http://www.washingtontimes.com/news/2009/jul/14/
ethics-probe-of-conyers-sought/.
18. http://www.freep.com/article/20090630/NEWS01/
90630022/John+Conyers+defends+waste-well+letter.
19. http://articles.cnn.com/2009-08-05/politics/us.rep
.trial_1_jefferson-aide-wire-fraud-rep-william-jeffer
son?_s=PM:POLITICS.
20. http://www.realclearpolitics.com/articles/2010/08/13/
race_card_payment_coming_due_106741.html.
21. http://thehill.com/blogs/floor-action/house/142929
-jackson-lee-blasts-demeaning-pepsi-super-bowl-ad.
22. http://www.mrc.org/bmi/articles/2009/Clyburn_
Stimulus_Refusal_A_Slap_in_the_Face_to_Blacks_
Even_if_Unintentional.html.

CHAPTER FIVE: THE NAACP AS
LIBERAL FRONT GROUP

1. http://online.wsj.com/article/SB100014240527023037
38504575568434291817928.html.
2. http://www.wallbuilders.com/LIBissuesArticles.asp?
id=122.
3. Ibid.
4. "Woodrow Wilson and White Supremacy: An Exami-
nation of Wilson's Racist and Antidemocratic Policies,"

Suite101.com, http://elvira-nieto.suite101.com/woodrow -wilson-and-white-supremacy-a126787#ixzz1abWo Nvhg.

5. http://www.academia.org/progressive-segregation/.
6. http://www.imdb.com/title/tt0004972/quotes.
7. http://www.pbs.org/wgbh/amex/wilson/portrait/wp_ african.html.
8. http://www.pbs.org/wnet/jimcrow/stories_events_tru man.html.
9. http://grandoldpartisan.typepad.com/blog/2007/05/ everett_dirksen.html.
10. http://newsbusters.org/blogs/noel-sheppard/2011/ 10/08/sharpton-doesnt-know-higher-percentage -republicans-democrats-voted-ci#ixzz1abDyk6ez.
11. http://newsone.com/nation/casey-gane-mccalla/al -sharpton-says-the-tea-party-is-antithetical-to-civil -rights/.
12. http://www.nationalcenter.org/P21PR-Tea_Party_ Tracker_090910.html.
13. http://dailycaller.com/2011/02/21/the-naacps-racism -double-standard/.
14. http://www.foxnews.com/opinion/2011/03/11/tea-party -movement-racism-lesson-npr-scandal/#ixzz1LOsbsr1k.

CHAPTER SIX: GREEN LIBERAL LIES

1. http://www.nytimes.com/cwire/2010/05/03/03 climatewire-sale-of-chicago-climate-exchange-to-ice -reinfo-362.html?pagewanted=all.

2. http://www.foxnews.com/politics/2010/11/09/collapse
   -chicago-climate-exchange-means-strategy-shift-global
   -warming-curbs/.
3. http://washingtonexaminer.com/politics/2009/08/
   leaked-e-mail-shows-how-ge-puts-government-work-ge
   #ixzz1Nr7iQ4Zw.
4. http://articles.latimes.com/print/2008/apr/14/nation/
   na-coalwars14.
5. http://www.nytimes.com/2011/07/22/nyregion/
   bloomberg-donates-50-million-to-sierra-club-coal-ca
   mpaign.html.
6. http://www.tennessean.com/fdcp/?unique=13049
   67355226.
7. http://www.recyclingfirst.org/blog/?post=111.
8. http://www.americaspower.org/news/new-analysis
   -shows-economic-damage-caused-epa-regulations
   -train-act-will-ensure-economic-conseq.
9. http://www.washingtonpost.com/wp-dyn/content/
   article/2010/12/30/AR2010123004304.html.
10. http://articles.sfgate.com/2011-01-09/business/27018
    705_1_coal-fired-power-coal-industry-coal-plants.
11. http://www.nytimes.com/gwire/2011/06/09/09
    greenwire-aep-predicts-need-to-shutter-25-of-coal
    -fleet-91911.html.
12. http://video.foxbusiness.com/v/4607794/obama
    -encourages-drillingin-brazil/.
13. http://www.nationalcenter.org/NPA622.html.
14. http://www.time.com/time/health/article/0,8599,20
    404085,00.html.

15. http://www.eia.gov/energy_in_brief/energy_subsidies .cfm.
16. http://www.thedailybeast.com/articles/2011/10/05/ americans-face-double-digit-hikes-in-electricity-bills -to-fund-upgrades.html.
17. http://www.whitehouse.gov/the-press-office/2011/ 01/25/remarks-president-state-union-address.
18. http://www.time.com/time/nation/article/0,8599,20 13683,00.html.
19. http://www.time.com/time/nation/article/0,8599,20 13683,00.html#ixzz1M4IedgyL.
20. http://www.earthtechling.com/2010/07/recovery -act-puts-over-90-billion-towards-clean-energy/.
21. http://articles.boston.com/2010-03-28/news/292 94966_1_weatherizing-energy-efficiency-job-goals.
22. "Obama's $5 Billion Weatherizing Program Wastes Stimulus Funds, Auditor Finds," Foxnews.com, April 14, 2011.
23. http://online.wsj.com/article/SB10001424052748703506 904575592843603174132.html?mod=googlenews_wsj.
24. http://green-states-news.greenpromote.biz/obama -streamlines-the-loan-guarantee-program/.
25. http://www.nma.org/statistics/fast_facts.asp.
26. http://www.eia.gov/neic/press/images/2010_13_figure 2.jpg.
27. http://www.instituteforenergyresearch.org/states/.
28. http://www.bloomberg.com/news/2010-06-24/ge-to -invest-10-billion-by-2015-under-immelt-s-ecomagina tion-plan.html.

29. http://www.clipsandcomment.com/2011/01/22/tran script-obama-weekly-address-january-22-2011-jobs -economy-china/.

30. http://washingtonexaminer.com/blogs/beltway -confidential/2011/02/new-soros-hedge-fun-profiting -obamas-green-energy-push-hires-top-#ixzzlG25 vlaZm.

31. http://www.ted.com/pages/view/id/50.

32. http://www.portfolio.com/executives/features/2007/ 03/29/Behind-the-Green-Doerr/.

33. Mark Hemingway, "Special Report—Big Green: Emanuel's Pot of Green Gold Is Called Exelon," *Washington Examiner,* September 28, 2010, http:// washingtonexaminer.com/node/524302.

34. http://news.medill.northwestern.edu/chicago/news .aspx?id=146431.

35. http://www.forbes.com/forbes/2010/0118/americas -best-company-10-exelon-utility-tax-carbon-windfall .html.

36. Dan Springer, "Energy in America: EPA Rules Force Shell to Abandon Oil," Foxnews.com, April 25, 2011, http://www.freerepublic.com/focus/f-news/2710093/ posts.

37. http://www.redstate.com/vladimir/2011/04/25/epa -ruling-kills-shells-plans-to-drill-offshore-alaska/.

38. http://www.fas.org/sgp/crs/misc/R40872.pdf.

39. http://dailycaller.com/2011/04/20/bp-benefitted-from -cozy-relationship-with-green-groups-and-the-media -before-oil-spill/.

40. Congressional Research Service, "U.S. Fossil Fuel Resources: Terminology, Reporting, and Summary," November 2010.

CHAPTER SEVEN: THE DANGERS OF AN UNHEALTHY LIBERAL AGENDA

1. http://millercenter.org/scripps/archive/speeches/detail/3418.
2. The Patient Protection and Affordable Care Act, Pub. L. No. 111-148 (2010); 124 Stat. 119 (HR 3590), available at http://www.gpo.gov/fdsys/pkg/PLAW-111publ148/pdf/PLAW-111publ148.pdf.
3. Health Care and Education Reconciliation Act of 2010, Pub. L. No. 111-152; 124 Stat. 1029 (HR 4872), available at http://www.gpo.gov/fdsys/pkg/PLAW-111publ152/pdf/PLAW-111publ152.pdf.
4. "Health Care Reform," *New York Times,* http://topics.nytimes.com/top/news/health/diseasesconditionsandhealthtopics/health_insurance_and_managed_care/health_care_reform/index.html (updated March 4, 2011).
5. Brian Blase, "Obamacare: The One-Year Checkup," Heritage Foundation, Backgrounder No. 2532, March 17, 2011, http://www.heritage.org/Research/Reports/2011/03/Obamacare-The-One-Year-Checkup.
6. For the results of Roll Call No. 165 for the House of Representatives vote on the Patient Protection and Affordable Care Act, visit http://www.congress.org/

congressorg/issues/votes/?votenum=165&chamber=H&
congress=1112. The more detailed results of the roll call
vote that lists each member, his or her party affiliation,
and vote on the legislation can be found at http://www
.congress.org/congressorg/issues/votes/?votenum=165&
chamber=H&congress=1112&tally=1.

7. http://www.cbsnews.com/8301-503544_162-6242715
-503544.html.

8. http://voices.washingtonpost.com/ezra-klein/2010/02/
obama_weve_got_to_go_ahead_and.html.

9. Jeffrey H. Anderson, "CBO: Obamacare Would Cost
Over $2 Trillion," *Weekly Standard,* March 18, 2010,
http://www.weeklystandard.com/blogs/cbo-obama
care-would-cost-over-2-trillion.

10. Ibid.

11. Merrill Matthews, "The Biggest Tax Increase in
U.S. History? The Justice Department Is Calling the
ObamaCare Mandate a Tax. If So, That's Bad News
for the President," Forbes.com, July 26, 2010, http://
www.forbes.com/2010/07/26/health-care-mandate
-barack-obama-opinions-contributors-merrill
-matthews.html.

12. Director Doug Elmendorf, Congressional Budget Office, testifying before the House Budget Committee,
reported in Jeffrey H. Anderson, "CBO Director Says
Obamacare Would Reduce Employment by 800,000
Workers," *Weekly Standard,* February 10, 2011, http://
www.weeklystandard.com/blogs/cbo-director-says
-obamacare-would-reduce-employment-800000-workers
_547288.html.

NOTES

13. http://blog.heritage.org/2011/01/12/half-of-all-states-now-suing-to-stop-obamacare/.
14. http://fixhealthcarepolicy.com/health-care-news/obamacare-dumps-millions-more-into-failing-medicaid-program/.
15. Chief Actuary Richard S. Foster, Department of Health and Human Services, "Estimated Financial Effects of the 'Patient Protection and Affordable Care Act,' as Amended," April 22, 2010, p. 3, available online at http://www.cms.gov/ActuarialStudies/Downloads/PPACA_2010-04-22.pdf.
16. Robert Pear, "Insurance Pools Readied in Some States," *New York Times,* June 26, 2010.
17. Letter from Douglas W. Elmendorf, Director, Congressional Budget Office, to Senator Michael B. Enzi, June 21, 2010, http://www.cbo.gov/ftpdocs/115xx/doc11572/06-21-High-Risk_Insurance_Pools.pdf.
18. Ibid.
19. John Boehner, "Republicans Support Better Solutions to Provide Coverage to Americans with Pre-Existing Conditions," January 25, 2011, http://johnboehner.house.gov/News/DocumentSingle.aspx?DocumentID=221321.
20. Sarah Kliff and J. Lester Feder, "Child-Only Health Plans Endangered," *Politico,* January 27, 2011, http://www.politico.com/news/stories/0111/48299.html (accessed March 10, 2011); U.S. Department of Health and Human Services, "Questions and Answers on Enrollment of Children Under 19 Under the New Policy That Prohibits Pre-Existing Condition Exclusions,"

October 13, 2010, http://www.hhs.gov/ociio/regula
tions/children19/factsheet.html (accessed March 16,
2011); Robert Pear, "U.S. to Let Insurers Raise Fees
for Sick Children," *New York Times*, October 13,
2010, http://www.nytimes.com/2010/10/14/health/
policy/14health.html (accessed March 8, 2011), cited
in Brian Blase, "Obamacare: The One-Year Checkup,"
Heritage Foundation, Backgrounder No. 2532, March
17, 2011, http://www.heritage.org/Research/Reports/
2011/03/Obamacare-The-One-Year-Checkup.

21. David Cordani, Chief Executive of the health insurer Cigna Corporation, quoted in Susan Heavey,
"Cigna CEO: Don't Repeal U.S. Health Law," Reuters
.com, November 9, 2010, http://www.reuters.com/
article/2010/11/09/us-summit-cigna-politics-idUS
TRE6A834D20101109.

22. David Redfern, Chief Strategy Officer, GlaxoSmith-
Kline, quoted in Susan Heavey, "Health Overhaul
Should Press Ahead: Industry," Reuters, November 11,
2010, available online at the Cato Institute at http://
www.cato-at-liberty.org/more-proof-obamacare-is-a
-sop-to-industry/.

23. Ibid.

24. "Why the Health Insurance Industry Supported
Obamacare," *The Covert Rationing Blog, Healthcare Rationing in America*, July 29, 2010, http://covertrationing
blog.com/weird-fact-about-insurance-companies/why
-the-health-insurance-industry-supported-obamacare.

25. John C. Goodman and Robert E. Moffit, "Solutions for the Ten Structural Flaws of Obamacare,"

Health Care News, Heartland Institute, April 1, 2011, http://www.heartland.org/healthpolicy-news.org/article/29441/Solutions_for_the_Ten_Structural_Flaws_of_Obamacare.html.

26. Ibid.
27. http://online.wsj.com/article/SB124567211118336815.html.
28. http://www.nytimes.com/2009/08/09/health/policy/09lobby.html.
29. http://washingtonexaminer.com/blogs/beltway-confidential/pelosi-health-care-039we-have-pass-bill-so-you-can-find-out-what-it039.
30. Drew Armstrong, "McDonald's, 29 other firms get health care coverage waivers," *USA Today*, October 7, 2010, http://www.usatoday.com/money/industries/health/2010-10-07-healthlaw07_ST_N.htm.
31. http://www.nypost.com/p/news/local/teachers_union_gets_pass_on_obamacare_dhoJQgXRKLwbYtp6Nam7LK.
32. Ibid.; Armstrong, "McDonald's, 29 other firms get health care coverage waivers."
33. Robert Pear, "Four States Get Waivers to Carry Out Health Law," *New York Times*, February 16, 2011, http://www.nytimes.com/2011/02/17/health/policy/17health.html?_r=1.
34. Ibid.
35. http://dailycaller.com/2011/05/17/nearly-20-percent-of-new-obamacare-waivers-are-gourmet-restaurants-nightclubs-fancy-hotels-in-nancy-pelosi%e2%80%99s-district/#ixzz1P4zipPOJ.

36. http://dailycaller.com/2011/06/17/obama-admin-to -end-health-care-waivers/#ixzz1SPJ7HyQ0.
37. http://www.gao.gov/products/GAO-11-725R.
38. http://www.marketwatch.com/story/firms-halting -coverage-as-reform-starts-survey-2011-06-06.
39. http://campaign2012.washingtonexaminer.com/blogs/ beltway-confidential/dean-employers-will-drop-cover age-under-obamacare.
40. "Health Care Law," Rasmussen Reports, May 9, 2011, http://www.rasmussenreports.com/public_content/ politics/current_events/healthcare/health_care_law.
41. John Boehner, "Boehner Floor Speech Opposing the Democrats' Government Takeover of Health Care," March 22, 2010, http://johnboehner.house.gov/News/ DocumentSingle.aspx?DocumentID=177587.
42. http://www.nytimes.com/2011/11/15/US/supreme -court-to-hear-case-challenging-health-law.html? pagewanted=all.

CHAPTER EIGHT: PLAYING THE RACE CARD

1. http://abcnews.go.com/blogs/politics/2011/08/rep -andre-carson-tea-party-wants-to-see-blacks-hanging -on-a-tree/.
2. http://www.washingtonpost.com/politics/maxine -waters-to-tea-party-go-to-hell/2011/08/22/gIQAjg EeWJ_story.html.
3. http://www.politico.com/blogs/click/0911/Morgan_ Freeman_Tea_party_is_racist.html.

CONCLUSION: UPRISING ON THE PLANTATION

1. http://www.nationalcenter.org/teapartysurvey.pdf.
2. http://newmediajournal.us/indx.php/item/1431.
3. http://www.reuters.com/article/2011/05/03/us-ge
   -green-idUSTRE7427F920110503.
4. FreedomWorks Activist Boot Camp 2011—Dean
   Clancy, Legislative Counsel and VP, Health Care
   Policy.
5. http://action.freedomworks.org/4662/cut-cap-balance
   -pledge?source=DCblog.
6. http://finance.yahoo.com/news/Nearly-half-of-US
   -households-apf-1105567323.html?x=0&.v=1.
7. http://www.freedomworks.org/scrapthecode/topten
   .php.
8. http://www.hebookservice.com/products/bookpage
   .asp?prod_cd=c6801#continue.

ACKNOWLEDGMENTS

As you read about my evolution from citizen to conservative activist, it will be clear that this book and my successes are a result of the help and support from many individuals.

To my parents, who gave me a solid foundation of moral and religious values and stepped in when necessary to give me a dose of reality and tough love.

To Tom, my soul mate, whose vision, wisdom, and unwavering source of encouragement and inspiration helped me recognize my potential. Thank you for helping me to step out way beyond my comfort zone.

To my key donors—Frayda and Ken Levy, Rebecca and Bill Dunn, Mary Beth and Dick Weiss, and Heather Higgins. Your generosity has allowed me the opportunity to work in public policy. If it were not for you, this book and my accomplishments would never have happened.

To Marlene Mieske, who kindly offered to host a fundraising reception for me in her home just moments after meeting me—thank you for your generosity and friendship.

To the Congress of Racial Equality's Roy Innis and Niger Innis, who gave me my first opportunity; the

National Center for Public Policy Research's Amy and David Ridenour, who hired me in a full-time position at Project 21; my dear friends Matt and Terry Kibbe, who put me on the national stage to speak before a million people at the 9/12 Tax Day Rally—thank you, all, for being risk-takers and taking a chance on a novice in public policy.

And speaking of risk-takers, my sincere gratitude to Roger Ailes, who hired me despite my lack of TV experience, and many thanks to the exceptional staff he has assembled at all levels at Fox News, including Suzanne Scott, Bill Shine, Sean Hannity, the anchors, the producers who book me, the production crew, and the hair and makeup personnel who make me look good!

To everyone at Simon & Schuster, including Carolyn Reidy, Louise Burke, Mitchell Ivers, Anthony Ziccardi, and Kristin Dwyer, thank you for making this book a reality.

To Glenn Beck for his courage and outstanding teaching ability and to the entire staff at Mercury Radio Arts Inc., including Joe Kerry, David Harsanyi, and Jon Miller.

To Maura Teitelbaum of Abrams Artists Agency for your vision and support.

To the Project 21 staff for your diligent support and friendship, including David Almasi, Mychal Massie, and Judy Kent.

To everyone at FreedomWorks who tirelessly fight for liberty and who have made Tom and me part of the FreedomWorks family, including Adam Brandon, Brendan Steinhauser, Dean Clancy, Wayne Brough, Russ Walker, and Kristina Ribali.

ACKNOWLEDGMENTS

To David Webb, Rev. C. L. Bryant, Giovanna Cugnasca, Steven Laboe, Billy Glynn, and my friends and supporters. I'm glad my experiences over the past six years brought us together.

Finally, to my dear fans and fellow Tea Party patriots—whom I've had the pleasure of meeting either personally or through social networking—whose continuous words of encouragement keep me going. Thank you, all.